Wilde

Wilde

Jonathan Fryer

HAUS PUBLISHING • LONDON

First published in Great Britain in 2005 by
Haus Publishing Limited
26 Cadogan Court
Draycott Avenue
London SW3 3BX

A CIP catalogue record for this book is available from the British Library

ISBN 1-904341-11-X

Designed and typeset in Garamond by Falcon Oast Graphic Art
Printed and bound by Graphicom in Vicenza, Italy

Front cover: courtesy of Akg Images
Back cover: courtesy of Akg-Images

For Inga Haag
so much more than a footnote to history

Contents

Introduction

Indiscretion is the better part of valour.

Although Oscar Wilde has been dead for more than a century, he is a strikingly modern figure. He was not just an acclaimed writer, undoubtedly the finest comic dramatist of his age; he was also a celebrity. His self-promotion, prior to his downfall, was relentless. He knew how to generate publicity, not just for his works, but also for himself, both through the newspapers and magazines of Victorian Britain and through gossip. As an Irishman, he was an outsider who managed to gatecrash London Society thanks to the gift of the gab, lashings of charm, and a few modest letters of introduction. Unlike many such interlopers and self-publicists, however, he had real talent. And unlike many talented men, he had a soul.

As a writer, Wilde is best known for his wit. His greatest comedy, *The Importance of Being Earnest*, sparkles and scintillates. Yet the skeleton of its plot would be absurd in another's hands. Dialogue gives the play its form, as well as holding the audience's attention, and what dialogue it is! But *The Importance of Being Earnest* is much more than a cavalcade of witticism; as with his other major plays, there is biting social satire behind the delightful repartee and froth. As Wilde's most comprehensive biographer, Richard Ellmann, astutely observed in the introduction to his *Oscar Wilde*, 'Essentially, Wilde was conducting, in the most civilized way, an anatomy of his society, and a radical reconsideration of its ethics. He knew all the secrets and could expose all the pretence. Along with Blake and Nietzsche, he was proposing that good and evil are not what they seem, and that moral tabs cannot cope with the complexity of behaviour.'

In short, Oscar Wilde was a philosopher, as well as a social analyst. He could easily have fulfilled those roles within the realms of academe; his studies at Trinity College, Dublin, and Magdalen College, Oxford, showed he had the brain for that. But like the TV historians of today, he wanted to bring his message to a much wider public than university undergraduates or the limited readership of academic tomes. Journalism was one obvious way of getting his ideas across, but in many ways it was too obvious. Rather than indulge in polemics (with some interesting exceptions, such as *The Soul of Man under Socialism*), he chose to convey his often revolutionary themes obliquely, through fiction and drama. Occasionally, as with Lord Henry Wotton in *The Picture of Dorian Gray*, a character is largely a dramatisation of himself, but more often he designed men and women who have a distinct personality, while furthering his dissident agenda.

Wilde is remembered as much for his life as he is for his work, a situation of which he would have thoroughly approved. As he himself declared to André Gide – and doubtless many others – *I have put my talent into writing, my genius I have saved for living*. For him, his life was a performance, often a brilliant performance; for much of the time, it was indeed as if he were on stage. His audiences came in three main types: high society, his intimate circle of friends, and last but not least, young male vagabonds, who fascinated him as much as he fascinated them.

The story of Oscar Wilde's life has the plot line of a black comedy in four acts. In the first, we see the young hero fashioning an identity for himself, trying out a series of poses – some more ridiculous than others – before settling on the vocation of social commentator. In the second act, he finds his true voice, not as a journalist, or as a poet, or even as a novelist (though he has tried all of these roles), but as a playwright. He enjoys huge success, both professionally and socially, yet already the stage is prepared for his nemesis. Not content with the late Victorian bourgeois idyll of a beautiful home, a loving wife, and two delightful children, he seeks the thrill of forbidden pleasures and the danger of disreputable company. He gives free rein to formerly dormant homosexual urges in acts of transgression that make him a criminal. The retribution of Act Three therefore comes as no surprise, as he is knocked off his pedestal by a baying public and sent to prison for two years. This proves in some ways to be a cathartic experience; in the final act we see a man who is beaten but unbowed, still a clown behind his mask of tragedy.

In the century since Oscar Wilde's death, his image has been constantly remade, which has added to the complexity of his legacy. In Britain, at least, his name was for a long time a byword for debauchery and disgrace, the perpetrator of a crime so horrible that one could not talk about it in polite society. Yet 100 years on, he is hailed as a hero, a martyr in the fight against bigotry and philistinism, as well as a gay icon. Of course, society has changed so fundamentally during this period that a revision of the prevailing judgements about Wilde was inevitable. What is remarkable is that the debate about his true importance still rages so furiously. Moreover, Wilde the social commentator is as influential today as he was in the Naughty Nineties – perhaps even more so. His values and his judgements are startlingly relevant to our contemporary world.

Wilde was of course a master of paradox, using the technique to signal truths that were otherwise difficult to perceive, rather as a Zen Buddhist might use the image of the sound of one hand clapping. His own character was a bundle of paradoxes: the ambitious artist who was also bent on his own destruction, the joker who saw the tragedy of reality, the sinner who was also a saint.

This makes him extremely hard to pin down. As he himself said, *The truth is never pure, and rarely simple*. But here are a few map references that might at least ease the journey of the reader who is in search of Oscar Wilde.

Jonathan Fryer
London

Educating Oscar

The aim of life is self-development.
To realise one's nature perfectly.

Oscar Fingal O'Flahertie Wills Wilde was born into notoriety. Both his parents ensured, by their character and their actions, that they would be the subjects of Dublin gossip. Each was a celebrity, in diverse ways, but they also had a distinctly ridiculous side, which was parodied mercilessly, foreshadowing Oscar's own public image: half genius, half clown.

Oscar's father, William Wilde (1815–1876), was a highly distinguished ear and eye specialist, a pioneer in his field. As his medical reputation grew, he attracted an ever more fashionable clientele, but he also made time to treat and operate on patients of much humbler origins. Instead of charging impoverished patients his usual professional fees, he would gather anecdotes and stories from them. These formed the raw material for many of his articles and books, which ranged in subject from medical treatises to Irish topography and folklore. He even penned a study of the Anglo-Irish satirist and clergyman, Jonathan Swift (1667–1745). In his prime, William Wilde was possessed of phenomenal mental as well as physical energy, though he was also subject to depression. Tasks that would have taken other men years, such as cataloguing a large collection of Irish antiquities, now housed in the National Museum of Ireland, he polished off at remarkable speed, accurately and elegantly.

William Wilde when young, from a drawing by J H Maguire, 1847

William Wilde remained a bachelor until his mid-30s, but that did not stop him fathering – and acknowledging – three illegitimate children, Henry, Emily and Mary, by at least two different women. He took a keen interest in his bastard offspring's development, and even had Henry trained as a surgeon, so they could work together in his practice. The two girls became wards of William's Protestant clergyman elder brother, Ralph, which demonstrates a notable degree of liberalism in the family, as well as Christian charity. Not surprisingly, William Wilde won the reputation of being something of a Lothario, despite the fact that he was physically unprepossessing, had a complexion that appeared permanently grubby, and displayed some distinctly unrefined personal habits. One smart lady dinner guest, the wife of a Lord Lieutenant, flatly refused to eat her soup chez Wilde, after her host had tested its temperature with his thumb.

Such foibles did not prevent him finding an apparently perfect love-match: Jane Francesca Elgee (1821–1896), whom he married in 1851. Despite her origins in the Protestant ascendancy, the Anglo-Irish minority who dominated Irish affairs from the 17th century onwards, Jane Wilde, like her husband, was passionately interested in things Irish. Indeed, to the dismay of some of her relatives, she became a fervent Irish nationalist, writing inflammatory poems in the nationalist cause, under the pen name Speranza. When some of these appeared in the late 1840s – painful memories of the sufferings and upheavals of the potato famine still alive in Irish minds – the unknown author of these rousing verses became an object of intense speculation. The British government suspected that the editor of the *Nation*, Gavan Duffy, was responsible, but when he was being tried for this and other alleged transgressions, Jane stood up in the public gallery and declared, 'I, and I alone, am the culprit, if culprit there be!' She was thereafter immensely proud of this act of heroism, which undoubtedly contributed to Gavan Duffy eventually being set free.

At 30, Jane Wilde was well beyond the normal threshold of matrimony for a woman of the period. Presumably, her husband knew what her real age was, but she habitually lied to other people about her date of birth. She would reduce her age by as much as five years, especially in candlelight. Standing nearly six feet tall in her stockinged feet, she towered over her husband, making the couple an obvious butt for cartoonists. Moreover, she accentuated her impressive appearance by wearing theatrical clothes, headdresses and jewellery.

Jane rising to fame as 'Speranza of the Nation' during the late 1840s: photgravure by Stephen Catterson Smith

As the years went by and her figure filled out, she became an increasingly absurd apparition. As she rarely rose before midday and shunned natural light, she was however able to stage-manage her appearances with the artful use of curtains and lampshades. Not that she minded being considered eccentric. Flamboyance and an impassioned rejection of bourgeois norms were natural conditions for a poet, she argued. Above all, she dreaded being regarded as respectable. She admitted frankly that she loved to make a sensation.

And as she told one young male visitor, much later in her life, 'When you are as old as I, young man, you will know that there is only one thing in the world worth living for, and that is sin.'

Such unconventional views, often expressed in extravagant terms, did not prevent Jane fulfilling her wifely duties. Soon after her marriage, she became pregnant, providing William with his first legitimate offspring, named William after himself, but forever referred to as 'Willie', who was born on 26 September 1852. Motherhood proved to be something of a shock for Jane, interrupting her routine, but she soon doted on the baby boy, perceiving nascent intellectual qualities, which she forecast could lead him to become the first President of an independent Ireland. Barely two years after Willie's birth, he was presented with a little brother, Oscar, who first saw the light of day on 16 October 1854, at the family's then home of 21 Westland Road, Dublin.

As a young man, Oscar claimed, with his mother's connivance, to have been born two years later. This deception grew out of a positively feminine vanity, as well as an apparent wish to make himself seem even more precocious than was the case. But it also allowed him to maintain falsely that he was born at 1 Merrion Square, a far smarter address, to which the Wilde family moved in 1855. This imposing residence, which survived the post-World War Two demolitions of Georgian Dublin and is now owned by an American college, was an ideal setting for Jane Wilde's new role as a society hostess. She and her husband between them had more than enough good connections in the intellectual and artistic worlds to guarantee a stimulating gathering. At dinner parties William Wilde would dominate the proceedings; he was witty and garrulous, and had such a rich fund of stories that guests were happy to sit listening to what was often a monologue. Indeed, he could become quite peevish if interrupted, or if someone else tried to take the upper hand. From quite an early age, both Willie and Oscar were allowed to sit at table when guests were present, providing they did not speak, and both learned from their father's power of oratory.

Jane Wilde came into her own at the large Saturday afternoon 'At Homes' that she instituted. These would often attract in excess of 100 visitors. Unusually for a society hostess, Jane was acknowledged as an intellectual equal by many of the men present. Fluent in several European languages, she was exceptionally well read. However, she did cause some mirth with her completely unfounded claims to some grand Italian lineage, suggesting that she was related to Dante. She would all too readily lapse into Italian, or make some sweeping continental gesture. She even pronounced her second son's name exotically, with the stress on the second syllable, OsCAR.

The upkeep of 1 Merrion Square required at least half a dozen servants, headed by a butler, as well as considerable expenditure. Oscar's childhood coincided with the zenith of William Wilde's professional success, when life seemed largely without problems. The doctor was able to command substantial fees from his more affluent clients. But he was profligate, acquiring various properties in different parts of Ireland that were hardly sound investments, as well as building an expensive house at Moytura, the site of a famous battle. At least these varied homes gave the family – which in 1857 had been augmented by a longed-for daughter, Isola – agreeable places to spend their holidays. Not that holidays were much different from the rest of the year, as far as the children were concerned. None of them went to primary school, as they were educated at home, by their parents and by French and German governesses.

Though perpetually busy, William Wilde was a devoted and loving father, and once Jane realised that the presence of three infants need not necessarily cramp her style, she began to savour the role of 'La Madre': the beloved mother who would raise a genius. For several years, she was convinced that genius would be Willie, but as her elder son became more reckless and disobedient, she transferred her ambitions to Oscar.

In May 1863, Willie was sent to St Columba's College near Dublin, in the hope that he would pay more attention to schoolmasters than he did to his governesses, but this experiment was not a success. Accordingly, in February 1864, he was transferred to Portora Royal School at Enniskillen, and Oscar went with him.

Oscar dressed modishly in the attire of a mid-Victorian child of the privileged classes

Oscar was only nine years old at the time, which was unusually young for this particular boarding school, but one presumes that the Wildes hoped that the two boys would keep an eye on each other. Willie, a boisterous and gregarious soul, settled in quickly. For Oscar the experience was less immediately attractive, and he tended to avoid talking about it in later life.

The year 1864 saw both triumphs and tragedy for William Wilde. He was knighted for services to medicine; he had also been named Surgeon Oculist in Ireland to Queen Victoria. Jane Wilde's republican sympathies were conveniently put aside, as she revelled in being Lady Wilde. Oscar was hugely proud, deriving as much pleasure from her title as she did. This juvenile snob would not lose his passion for titles until his downfall 31 years later. However, the Wildes' joy at their social elevation was short-lived, as William Wilde found himself at the centre of a terrible scandal. A 28-year-old patient of his, Mary Travers, claimed that he had drugged her and raped her two years previously. Her case was weak, not least because she had chosen to remain on Dr Wilde's books after the alleged incident. However, during 1864, Miss Travers started to write damaging letters to the newspapers, and published a scurrilous pamphlet about Sir William and Lady Wilde. Jane, who dismissed Miss Travers's accusations as preposterous, was so incensed about the slur on the family's reputation that she sued for libel. The case went against her, and although Mary Travers was awarded only a farthing in damages – a damning indictment of her supposedly violated innocence – the Wildes were left with a colossal legal bill. Colleagues of Sir William, on both sides of the Irish Sea, rallied round in sympathy. But the scandal undoubtedly besmirched his public reputation.

One cannot know just how much young Oscar got to hear about the affair while he was at Portora, but given the nature of schoolboys, it is unlikely that he would have escaped a degree of ragging over it. Nonetheless, in contrast to Willie, he was starting to show academic prowess. In 1866, he did so well in the junior school that he was exempted from taking the end-of-year examinations. He began to develop a profound interest in the literature and history of ancient Rome and Greece. He became a discriminating student, in that he knew what interested him, but he could not be bothered to apply himself to things that did not. He had inherited his father's academic facility, quickly grasping the essence of a subject. He was also a natural speed-reader. But unlike Willie, who threw himself into sport and enjoyed taking part in musical events, Oscar showed little talent for fitting in. As his school years progressed, he deliberately stressed his otherness by choosing to wear shirts of scarlet and lilac, befitting a dandy in the making.

He also began to write verse. One of his earliest poems was occasioned by the sudden death of his sister Isola, as the age of nine, in February 1867. Oscar was very fond of Isola, seeing her almost as a symbol of young innocence, and his poem 'Requiescat', though redolent of Victorian sentimentality, also communicates real grief, beginning:

> *Tread lightly, she is near*
> *Under the snow*
> *Speak gently, she can hear*
> *The lilies grow.*

Lady Wilde declared melodramatically that she would never go to another dinner or soirée again, so devastating was the loss of her only daughter. Sir William also said that Isola's death left him a mourner for life. Even worse pain awaited him, as his other two daughters, Emily and Mary, both died horribly in November 1871 as a result of burns sustained when their dresses accidentally caught fire while they were preparing to go out to a party. Sir William was inconsolable, and from then on went into decline.

The tragedy of his half-sisters' deaths took some of the shine off Oscar's great achievement in that year of 1871: winning a scholarship to Trinity College, Dublin, a distinction enhanced by an exhibition award from Portora. He certainly left the school in a blaze of glory, though the moment of actual departure was burned into his consciousness for an entirely different reason. He had become close friends with another pupil, who was a year or two younger. They had often gone on long walks together, talking interminably. The boy went to the railway station to bid Oscar farewell, and as the Dublin train was about to depart, he suddenly exclaimed, 'Oh, Oscar!', took Oscar's face between his hot hands and kissed him on the lips. The 16-year-old Oscar had probably not had any physical relationship with anyone at school, but now he realised with a shock that he could be loved by another male.

Trinity College was, and remains, at the heart of Dublin's intellectual life. It was the obvious place for Oscar to go to further his academic studies. His brother Willie was already there and Oscar knew many of the teaching faculty, as they attended his mother's salon. That included the tutor to whom he was assigned, the Reverend John Pentland Mahaffy, a self-opinionated but brilliant teacher of ancient history, who had a particular passion for the Greeks.

They were, he argued, the instigators of much of what was noble in Western civilization. While in no way endorsing homosexual practices, Mahaffy championed the Greek ideal of intense relationships between men and youths, which could, he believed, surpass the love between a man and a woman. Though no such relationship developed between Mahaffy and Oscar, the tutor did communicate to his pupil his zeal for all things Hellenic. Mahaffy had eclectic interests, including a taste for foreign travel, fine wines and *objets d'art*, and he was a brilliant, if combative, conversationalist. Perhaps his greatest shortcoming was that he wrote nowhere near as dazzlingly as he spoke.

John Pentland Mahaffy (1839–1919) was a translator of and commentator on the German philosopher Immanuel Kant (1724–1804). However, his real passion was for the history and literature of ancient Greece. Once installed as Professor of Ancient History at Trinity College, Dublin, he became a scourge of Irish nationalists, accusing them of provincialism. He derided the Gaelic language, once declaring that it was impossible to find any Gaelic literature that was not religious, silly or indecent. He became Provost of Trinity College in 1914, and was knighted four years later. Though Oscar Wilde was one of his protégés, he refused to speak about him after the trials.

Politically, Oscar reacted against Mahaffy, rather than being influenced by his views. Mahaffy was a Unionist of the High Tory kind, whereas Oscar had adopted his mother's nationalist sympathies. But politics were not uppermost in his mind. At Trinity, Oscar usually eschewed political debates, in favour of more aesthetic discourse. He devoured the poetry of Algernon Swinburne (1837–1909), and was excited to read the views of John Addington Symonds (1840–1893), who declared that, 'Guided by no supernatural revelation, with no mosaic law for conduct, [the Greeks] trusted their *aesthetic*, delicately trained and preserved in a condition of the utmost purity.'[1] For the young Oscar, this was a deeply appealing take on morality, which would help lay the foundations for his own personal code of behaviour. He wrote a fan letter to Symonds, and a correspondence ensued, unfortunately lost to posterity. During his lifetime, Symonds received many such letters of 'avowal' from young men, who recognised echoes of their own sentiments in his writings. These writings became progressively more overt in their propagation of what he termed the 'love of the impossible', in other words, the love of an older man for a youth. For a while, Symonds tried to suppress his own sexual nature through marriage and fatherhood, but later he came ruefully to the conclusion that his whole life had been a lie.

Though Oscar continued to live mainly at home during his time at Trinity, he did for a while occupy undistinguished rooms in a college building called Botany Bay, where he could entertain guests privately and could ostentatiously display his modest efforts as a visual artist. He had started sketching while he was still at school, and would sometimes illustrate letters to his parents with caricatures of his classmates, but he could not claim great talent with either pen or brush. Nonetheless, he already had a well-developed artistic sensibility, proclaiming a special appreciation of Pre-Raphaelites such as Sir Edward Burne-Jones (1833–1898), whose virginal damsels with alabaster faces and flowing locks became Oscar's template of feminine beauty. Few of his acquaintances in Dublin shared such tastes, which led Oscar to realise that however rich Irish folklore and brilliant some Irish conversation might be, his native city was largely inhabited by Philistines.

Several times at Trinity, Oscar demonstrated his academic prowess. He won the Berkeley Gold Medal for Greek and did well enough in his final examinations in the summer of 1874 to make a career in academe a possibility. There was, however, no guarantee that he would be awarded a fellowship at Trinity if he decided to stay on. Besides, Professor Mahaffy was of the opinion that it would do Oscar good to go over the water to read for another undergraduate degree. He was still not yet 20.

By moving to England, Oscar was once again following in his brother Willie's footsteps. Willie was by then training to be a lawyer at the Middle Temple in London. Lady Wilde hoped that this might lead him towards a parliamentary future. She was not quite sure what she wanted for her younger son, but she did think it would help if he broadened his horizons. In late June, she travelled with him to England, where he sat an examination for a scholarship in classics at Magdalen College, Oxford. He was able to celebrate his success in this with his mother and brother, not just in London, which Lady Wilde declared to be 'the capital of the world'[2], but also on a holiday in Switzerland and France, thus giving Oscar his first taste of Paris.

When Oscar went up to Oxford that October, he was determined to make his mark. At 6'3", he literally stood out among the other students, and he accentuated his otherness by behaving with supreme self-confidence. He spoke with a marked Irish accent – which largely disappeared as the years went by – and dressed in loud or startling clothes that were guaranteed to provoke. He fell in with a set of mainly affluent young men who took boisterous pleasure much more seriously than they did academic study. For a brief period, Oscar took up sport, including boxing and rowing, before deciding that it was a pointless occupation. Under the influence of one friend, Courtenay Bodley, he also became a Mason, which must have pleased Sir William Wilde, who had been Master of the Shakespeare Lodge in Dublin. Spending too much time on extra-curricular activities and cavorting with boon companions quickly took its toll, however, as Oscar did shamefully badly by failing his first academic test, Responsions, the preliminary examinations in Classics, at the end of November 1874. He was formally reprimanded by Magdalen College's President, Frederick Bulley, for failing to live up to expectations. This was a salutary lesson, and in future he would study hard, well out of sight of his fellows, while publicly maintaining a façade of academic insouciance.

Of course, Oscar enjoyed the great advantage of having spent three years at Trinity studying many of the Greek and Roman authors who were once again on his syllabus. This enabled him to devote a considerable amount of his study-time to broadening his knowledge in more modern European philosophy and literature. In a commonplace book and other notebooks, he jotted down quotations that particularly struck him, and he began to log his own aphorisms – precursors to the witty epigrams that would become one of his most enduring legacies. He thought about them and he polished them, and like an artist trying out his sketches on the public, he would bring out the best of them on parade in his conversation.

As intended, some of his best remarks featured in university gossip. The most successful quip was born out of Oscar's purchase of blue china, including a pair of vases to hold the lilies that had become a trademark of his interior decoration. He once declared – or more likely, several times – that he found it 'harder and harder to live up to my blue china'. This remark was already circulating in 1876; subsequently, the vicar of St Mary's Church, Oxford, preached a sermon against the heathen sentiments that lay behind it. Even after Oscar had left Oxford, his saying had resonance, as it appeared, only slightly modified, in a cartoon in the satirical magazine *Punch* in October 1880.

From his first year at Oxford, Oscar entertained generously. He held open house in his rooms on Sunday evenings, after supper, at which guests could help themselves to tureens of gin and whisky punch, as they talked late into the night. Oscar began to run up large bills with various tradesmen in the town, who allowed students to buy things on account. Having known in his childhood a period in which his family were at the height of their fortunes, he seems to have been unable to recognise that their situation had deteriorated seriously since. Exhausted, demoralised and increasingly unwell, Sir William practised less and less, which meant that his income was only a fraction of what it had been. He had even had to take a mortgage out on 1 Merrion Square. But Oscar at Oxford felt he had an image to keep up, and the wealth and profligacy of most of his friends did not encourage frugality.

His best friend at university was a young man called Hunter Blair, a Scottish baronet who owned substantial property. Blair often accompanied Oscar on his shopping expeditions. In the Easter vacation of 1875, Blair travelled to Italy, where he converted to Roman Catholicism, and on his return to Magdalen, he tried to persuade several of his friends to follow suit. Oscar was in many ways an obvious candidate for conversion. Rumour had it that his mother had actually secretly had him baptised into the Church of Rome when he was an infant. Moreover, Oscar was fascinated by Catholic ritual. But Sir William made it very clear that if Oscar became a Catholic, he would disinherit him. Oscar nonetheless continued to flirt with Rome for the rest of his life.

Strangely, when Oscar had the opportunity to visit Italy in the summer of 1875, he made no effort to visit the Eternal City. Travelling for much of the time with his old Trinity tutor John Mahaffy and another young Dubliner, William Goulding, he visited Florence, Bologna and Venice, before moving on to Verona and Padua. He sent enthusiastic missives home to his father, extolling the beauty of the art and architecture he saw there. He was well primed for the visit, having attended over the previous months a series of lectures on Florentine art given at the University Museum by the great critic John Ruskin (1819–1900). Ruskin became a mentor as well as a friend, though Oscar would soon reject many of Ruskin's moral judgements. Meanwhile, the sights and sounds of Italy acted as muses to Oscar's poetic voice. He sent some of his verses back to his mother, receiving in return a typical snippet of critical advice, after his poem 'San Miniato' was published in the university magazine: 'Sin is respectable and highly poetical. *Shame* is not.'[3]

When he started to run out of money, he headed home to Ireland, via Paris. During August, he was able to enjoy the boating and fishing at Moytura House, by Lough Corrib. Here he had his first romantic attachment with a young lady, Florence

Balcombe, the exquisitely pretty (but, sadly, not rich) 17-year-old daughter of an English Lieutenant-Colonel. The two sweethearts kept in touch when Oscar returned to Oxford, and at Christmas he presented her with a gold cross. Oscar loved the idea of being in love with such a beautiful girl. But his ardour, if ardour it was, could not be sustained at a distance and they drifted apart. Florence later became an actress, and married Bram Stoker (1847–1912), the future creator of Dracula.

Back at Magdalen, Hunter Blair kept up the pressure on Oscar to convert. Oscar attended the dedication ceremony at St Aloysius Church in St Giles, presided over by Cardinal Henry Manning (1808–1892), who Oscar allowed was deeply impressive. But to Hunter Blair's exasperation Oscar declared that he was vacillating between Roman Catholicism and Atheism. This was not the only vacillation in his life. Indeed, one of his most enduring characteristics was that he wanted things both, if not all, ways.

Nowhere was this more evident than in Oscar's growing awareness of his bisexuality. He loved to flirt with women and to arouse

Oscar strikes a determinedly languid pose, later aped by generations of would-be aesthetes on both sides of the Atlantic

their emotions, but he was also developing his feminine side. This self-feminisation went far beyond a certain aesthetic preciousness. He grew his hair conspicuously long, and to the dismay of some of his heartier friends, he started to move, as well as talk, in an increasingly unmanly fashion. By accident or design, he extended his circle of acquaintances to include other young men who were attracted by the Greek ideal of passionate, but often physically chaste, relationships between men and youths. Oscar was not alone in committing to verse an adoration of beautiful boys, in his case, invariably pale-skinned, rose-lipped and with hair of gold. One such sonnet he had published in the Trinity College magazine *Kottabos* in 1877, though he changed the sex of the object of his attention when the poem was included in his later volume of poems. There is no evidence to suggest that Oscar consummated his homosexual urges at this stage, but like many Oxford undergraduates at the time, he liked to talk about the subject, or to gossip about other students or dons who had been seen in public with pretty choirboys.

Determined to keep open the option of becoming a don himself, Oscar stayed on in Oxford during the spring vacation of 1876, to swot for examinations due in June. But soon he found himself summoned to Dublin, where his father was dying. Sir William passed away on 19 April, the grief of his death compounded by the alarming state of the family finances, as was revealed when his will was read. Willie inherited 1 Merrion Square and Lady Wilde, Moytura House, but both were heavily mortgaged, as well as being expensive to maintain. Oscar got some small and not particularly valuable houses in Bray, which were rented out, and a half-share – with his half-brother Henry – in a lodge at Illaunroe on Lough Fee in Connemara. This was all very vexing. Nonetheless, he applied himself well enough to his classical studies to get a First in his second year examinations, though he ploughed his concomitant test in Divinity, refusing to take it seriously. He behaved with insolence towards his Divinity examiner, the legendary Dr William Spooner

(1844–1930). In fact, Oscar treated most of his tutors and the university authorities with disdain.

Undeterred by Oscar's spiritual promiscuity and renewed interest in Freemasonry, Hunter Blair persuaded him to join him in Rome in the spring vacation of 1877, even covering most of Oscar's expenses. Oscar travelled from London to Genoa with John Mahaffy, who then succeeded in diverting Oscar to Greece. As Mahaffy had hoped, Athens and other Hellenic sites made a deep impression on Oscar. But he felt guilty about keeping Hunter Blair waiting in Rome. Accordingly, he sailed over to Italy in late April. Hunter had a genuine surprise in store there: a private audience with Pope Pius IX (1792–1878), an experience that, for once, left Oscar dumbstruck.

He returned to Oxford more than three weeks late for the start of term, an act of nonchalant defiance that resulted in his being rusticated – in other words, barred from the city – until October, as well as having some of his scholarship docked. Professor Mahaffy and Lady Wilde were both outraged at his treatment.

Oscar stopped off in London en route for Dublin, pausing long enough to visit the Grosvenor Gallery in New Bond Street, which had been established specifically to exhibit works by the Pre-Raphaelites and other painters excluded from the Royal Academy. Oscar wrote a review of the Grosvenor Gallery show – his first published piece of prose – for the Dublin University Magazine, and decided that the vocation of art critic would suit him admirably. He sent a copy

Oscar in his student tweeds at Oxford

The son of a doctor who had dedicated much of his life to serving the poor, Walter Pater (1839–1894) became sensitive to art and architecture while a schoolboy at King's School, Canterbury. He spent most of his life in the ivory towers of Oxford, reading voraciously and extending his academic interests into the fields of literature and philosophy. He abandoned plans to become an Anglican priest, instead devoting himself to teaching and writing. Oscar Wilde was attracted by Pater's credo that one should 'burn with a hard, gem-like flame', but Pater's reputation in late-Victorian England suffered as fellow academics and critics increasingly suspected him of hedonism, or worse.

of the article to Walter Pater (1839–1894), whose writings on art and aesthetics had largely displaced Ruskin from Oscar's intellectual affections.

Pater responded promptly to Oscar's letter, urging him to call on him when he returned to Oxford. Oscar duly did so in October, having paved the way for this first meeting by sending Pater several sonnets. 'Why do you always write poetry?' Pater admonished him. 'Why do you not write prose? Prose is so much more difficult.'[4]

Deeply influenced by his friends among the Pre-Raphaelites, Pater re-evaluated what he saw as true Hellenism and medieval sensibility; his *Studies in the History of the Renaissance* would become a handbook for a new generation of Oxford aesthetes, even if some of their peers questioned the desirability of some of the ideas he propagated. It was from Pater that Oscar learned the important lesson that a good work of art does not have to be moral. Pater had quite a soft spot for what he called 'refined and comely decadence'. In that sense, he was quite

revolutionary, though he was discomforted by just how far Oscar was prepared to push beyond the frontiers of the conventionally acceptable. At times it seemed as if Pater was scared of letting himself go, though in principle he approved of the notion of living from sensation to sensation.

Oscar's fourth year at Oxford was his most brilliant, as he worked hard to ensure that he would get a First Class degree. Simultaneously, he composed the long poem that he would enter for the much coveted Newdigate Prize, established in the 18th century by the antiquary Sir Roger Newdigate to reward the best undergraduate piece of English verse. John Ruskin and Matthew Arnold figured among earlier laureates. Fortuitously, the subject set for the 1878 competition was Ravenna, a city that Oscar had visited on his second trip to Italy. Profoundly superstitious, Oscar handed in his manuscript on 31 March, a year to the day of his entering Ravenna. Though somewhat disjointed in its themes, the poem nonetheless has echoes of authentic experience. It won the approval of the judges, who awarded him the prize. His public reading of 'Ravenna' in late June was warmly applauded. And with the announcement of his final examination results, his triumph was complete: a double first, having won first class honours in both Moderations in July 1876 and his final examinations.

There were a few clouds on his horizon, however, not least the fact that his failure to pass obligatory examinations in Divinity meant that he would have to return to Oxford in the autumn to sit them again. Several creditors, mainly Oxford tradesmen, were hounding him. Lady Wilde's exhortation that both he and Willie should try to marry rich heiresses made a lot of sense. In the meantime, there remained the vexed question of what he would actually do now his formal studies were coming to an end. When pressed on the matter by Hunter Blair, Oscar replied with prescience, *I'll be a poet, a writer, a dramatist. Somehow or other, I'll be famous, and if not famous, notorious.*[5]

Exquisitely Being

There is only one thing in the world worse than being talked about, and that is not being talked about.

Whatever Oscar was going to do, he was determined to do it in London. He had outgrown the provincialism of Dublin and his efforts to prolong yet further his time in Oxford, through some academic appointment, were decidedly half-hearted. London, as well as being the metropolis of a great and growing Empire, was the place where most of the really important people in Britain lived, and it was the unchallenged literary and artistic centre.

Oscar was fortunate in finding lodgings with an affluent young artist friend of his, Frank Miles, at 13 Salisbury Street, off the Strand. He was thus admirably placed for forays to the theatre, art exhibitions and fashionable restaurants. No longer needing to do any serious academic study, Oscar was able to become a dilettante, a young man of leisure whose days were filled with long conversations over cigarettes and drinks with Frank Miles and visiting friends, discussing pictures they had seen or debating at length where they would go out to eat. In stark contrast to the prevailing protestant work ethic that drove Victorian industry and progress, Oscar's motivation was to live life to its full, in particular savouring the artistic and culinary opportunities of the most dynamic city in the world. He would later make light of the self-indulgent existence of gentlemen of independent means and those, like himself, who determined to live it though they could not really afford to do so, with his quip that *work is the curse of the drinking classes*. But he believed that the pursuit of enjoyable experiences was a matter that should be treated as seriously as any career.

Lord Ronald Gower, a notorious practitioner of the credo of living entirely for pleasure, with a particular taste for men in uniform, had first brought Miles to visit Oscar in Oxford in 1875, and a friendship had quickly developed. Though Miles was predominantly interested in young girls – the age of consent in those days being 13 – he was not averse to the flattering attention of men like Gower, who were attracted by his striking good looks, nor to engaging in badinage with Oscar about both pure and impure Greek longings for beautiful youths. Beauty was what bound Oscar and Frank Miles together and they determined that their household in Salisbury Street, in which they occupied separate floors, would be a temple to it. Miles sketched many lovely women there, notably actresses, models and young Society ladies, who were dubbed the Professional Beauties, or PBs, and he enjoyed considerable commercial success with the results. Edward, Prince of Wales – who had a famously sharp eye for the girls – was one of his clients and would sometimes call, especially if his current mistress, Lillie 'Jersey Lily' Langtry, was going to be there.

Oscar was smitten by Lillie Langtry and kept a portrait of her on an easel as the focal point of his rooms, which were all painted white – a daring decorative innovation for the age. He showered praise and bunches of lilies on her, and was said to have slept on her doorstep to catch a glimpse of her as she came home. The lilies were not just an unsubtle reference to her sobriquet, but also a symbol of purity, which was deliciously inappropriate in her case. Other female beauties, 'professional' or otherwise, were also beneficiaries of Oscar's intemperate floral gifts, including the actresses Sarah Bernhardt and Ellen Terry. These women were flattered by the extravagance of his often highly public gestures,

Emily Charlotte 'Lillie' Langtry (1853–1929) was forever in the gossip columns. Photographs and reproductions of the numerous portraits of her made her one of the first 'pin-up' girls. The daughter of a clergyman from the Channel Islands, she used her guile, as well as her looks, to propel herself into higher spheres. Frank Miles, along with fellow artists Whistler and Millais, was captivated by her at a soirée in Spring 1877, and her reputation was launched overnight. Her affair with Prince Edward lasted three years, after which she became pregnant by Prince Louis of Battenberg. When King Edward died, Lillie inherited his favourite dog.

while recognising him to be sexually unthreatening. He adored them and paid homage to them, but he made it clear that for him, sublime happiness would not be to bed them, but rather to write a play worthy of having one of them star in it. In the meantime, Oscar took on the role of Lillie Langtry's part-time, unpaid mentor, teaching her Latin, advising her on her dress, and helping to promote her among the London public, knowing that in doing so, he was also promoting himself. He was also largely responsible for persuading her that the best way to overcome her relative penury was to go onto the stage.

Oscar's first play, *Vera; Or, The Nihilists*, was completed in early 1880. Showing himself to be truly the son of 'Speranza' Wilde, he chose a highly political, indeed republican, theme. The plot concerns an assassination attempt on the Czar in turn-of-the-19th-century Russia. There are many glaring anomalies and inconsistencies in this juvenile four-acter, showing that the author had done little serious research into Russian history. But in the drama's challenge to the maintenance of imperial power and inherited privilege, there are interesting echoes of primitive socialism, as well as nihilism, the belief that all values are baseless and that nothing can be known for certain, suggesting that Oscar was using the play as a means of experimenting with his own political ideas. The fact that some of these were blatantly contradictory was in keeping with Oscar's own complex, developing persona. He was happy to hobnob with Tory aristocrats, while openly wooing the attention of the grand old man of the Liberal Party, William Gladstone, and studying far more outlandish creeds, including early socialist writings and oriental philosophy. Such intellectual promiscuity, coupled with wit, meant that Oscar was seen by many of his acquaintances as an amusing but shallow fraud. In fact, he did have a developed social consciousness, and even as he clambered up the greasy pole of London Society, he would take time off to visit the poor in South London to understand the dreadful living and working conditions of London's huge under-class and bring them succour, sometimes in material handouts, but more often in the form of sympathetic concern.

Oscar was pleased to discover how easy it was to penetrate London Society if one had determination, good connections and, above all, style. Money and titles were all very well, particularly when the serious subject of marriage was at stake, but at other times Society ladies had a struggle to keep ennui at bay. Someone who could make them laugh, maybe even be a little shocking, without being offensive, was highly prized. Moreover, Oscar's mother and brother soon became champions of his social and literary promise. They had disposed of their Irish properties and set up house in London, first in Ovington Square and then in Park Street, Mayfair, where Lady Wilde hosted a salon, not quite as grand as the one she had presided over in Ireland, but nonetheless interesting and eclectic. Willie stumbled into journalism, and proved to be rather good at it; having few moral scruples, he saw nothing wrong in giving his younger brother generous 'puffs' in gossip columns. Moreover, Oscar, the budding playwright, could be paraded before Speranza's guests, and his cultivated, even cheeky nonchalance made an intriguing contrast to the nervous earnestness of other putative literary lion cubs. One gets the flavour of Oscar's bravado from a letter he wrote to Edward Smyth-Pigott, Examiner of Plays for the Lord Chamberlain, when he submitted Vera for comment: *I am working at dramatic art because it's the <u>democratic</u> art, and I want fame, so any suggestion, any helpful advice, your experience and very brilliant critical powers can give me I shall thank you very much for.*[6]

By this time, the late summer of 1880, Oscar and Frank Miles – thanks to the latter's relative wealth – had moved to much more fitting surroundings for young men about town: an artistic dwelling in Tite Street, Chelsea, a part of town that was attracting growing numbers of young men and women who were part of, or attracted by, what later became known as the Aesthetic Movement. Though the Aesthetic Movement had precursors in poets such as John Keats (1795–1821) and Percy Bysshe Shelley (1792–1822) and some of the Pre-Raphaelite painters, it was largely Walter Pater's critical essays that helped shape the aesthetic ideal of leading figures in the Movement, including Oscar Wilde. The French philosopher, Victor Cousin (1792–1867) had coined the phrase 'Art for Art's sake', which became a rallying cry for those who believed that it was not necessary for a beautiful object or painting or piece of writing to have any moral message – thereby overturning one of the central assumptions of Victorian orthodoxy. Beauty was perfect in itself, and one should happily become a follower of the cult of beauty. What is more, Art should not try to emulate Life; Life should copy Art. This philosophy of life inevitably affected the way an Aesthete would decorate his home, the clothes he would wear, even the way he would behave.

The Tite Street house was refurbished for Miles by the fashionable aesthetic architect and designer Edward Godwin (1833–1886), who had created a nearby studio for James McNeill Whistler, The White House, three years previously. Oscar grandly gave his new home the name Keats House, though it had no connection whatsoever with the poet. Despite the 20 year gap in their ages, Oscar and Whistler – who had moved into another house in Tite Street, after losing The White House through debts incurred through a disastrous libel action against John Ruskin – became good friends, admiring each other's talent and wit, and sharing a disdain for the philistinism of bourgeois society, though Whistler from the beginning considered Oscar to be something of an upstart.

Rather like an old lion looking warily at a younger potential rival, Whistler would keep slapping Oscar down when he felt he was taking himself too seriously. Oscar genuinely admired Whistler at first, but as the years went by, he became ever more conscious of the older man's vanity and unpredictability. It took some time for him to realise that one of Whistler's characteristics was to turn on friends after some perceived slight, and then behave as if they were enemies. Whistler admitted openly that he enjoyed cultivating enemies.

The artist James Abbott McNeill Whistler (1834–1903) spent part of his childhood in the Russian capital, St Petersburg, while his father was working on building the railway to Moscow. He resolved to be an artist and in 1855 – aged only 21 – headed for Paris, where he rubbed shoulders with Charles Baudelaire, Gustave Courbet and Edouard Manet. He moved to London four years later, winning a high reputation for his sometimes contentious art, which showed enormous versatility, from the subtlety of his Thames 'Nocturnes' to the rich decorative inventiveness of the Peacock Room.

For the time being, however, their very public friendship and loud repartee attracted considerable media attention, sometimes flattering, but often derisive, as cartoonists and satirists lampooned the aesthetic ideal for being out of keeping with vigorous Victorian masculinity. A former Parisian classmate of Whistler's, the artist and future novelist George du Maurier (1834–1896), created a whole series of monstrous figures in the satirical magazine *Punch* which were clearly based on Oscar and his mannerisms. There was no attempt on du Maurier's part to hide the identity of his caricatures' origin, as they boasted such names as Oscuro Wildegoose and Ossian Wilderness. While Oscar was sometimes irritated by the shallowness of the parody, he nonetheless recognised how useful such exposure was for his campaign of self-promotion.

Worse, or maybe one should say better, was to come. During the winter of 1880–1881, William Gilbert (1836–1911) worked on the libretto of a comic opera, *Patience*, in which he sent up the whole aesthetic movement. Although the principal aesthetic character, Bunthorne, has some of Whistler's characteristics, many of his utterances and poses are indubitably based on Oscar. At one moment, Bunthorne declares, 'It is the wail of the poet's heart on discovering that everything is commonplace, to understand it, cling passionately to one another and think of faint lilies.'[7] The opera, with music by Arthur Sullivan (1842–1900) opened in London on 23 April 1881, in a production by Richard D'Oyly Carte (1844–1901), to general public mirth. It was hard for Oscar to find the correct, dignified reaction, so he affected to be unconcerned.

Besides, he had more important things on his mind. He was only too aware that he had created something of a reputation for himself without having done very much – a situation that needed to be rectified. He had sent copies of his play *Vera* to various people connected with the theatre, but it had elicited little enthusiasm. Accordingly, he decided to try another tack and produce a volume of poetry. He had already managed to place about 30 poems in magazines, and had an equal number of unpublished verses, which meant that he had enough to fill a slight book. Just as he had had *Vera* privately printed, so now he approached the small publisher David Bogue, and signed a contract with him by which Oscar would be responsible for all the costs of publication. The initial edition of *Poems* was for 250 copies, though the book was later reprinted several times. Roberts Brothers in Boston produced an American edition. Oscar was very particular about the book's appearance, specifying Dutch handmade paper and a white parchment binding.

There are echoes of adolescence and Oxford in *Poems*, though it is also a book reflecting Oscar's transition into maturity and the London environment. Many of the poems are romantic in tone, but they are uneven in style as well as mood. At times it is as if the author is expressing a world- weariness way beyond his years. The opening poem, 'Hélas!' (Alas!), even contains an element of self-rebuke:

> *To drift with every passion till my soul*
> *Is a stringed lute upon which all winds can play,*
> *Is it for this that I have given away*
> *Mine ancient wisdom and austere control?*

The diversity of style and inconsistency of themes in the book made it difficult for many readers to judge it. There was something to please and to offend almost everyone, especially in the poems' vacillation between religious and pagan standpoints. Christian readers who might happily endorse the piety and penitence expressed in a poem such as 'San Miniato' would be brought up with a jolt by the unalloyed sensuousness of the long sequence 'Charmides', which begins:

> *He was a Grecian lad, who coming home*
> *With pulpy figs and wine from Sicily*
> *Stood at his galley's prow, and let the foam*
> *Blow through his crisp brown curls unconsciously . . .*

The book was ready at the very end of June or early July. In keeping with the custom of the times, Oscar fired off copies not just to friends, but also to other writers, influential critics and public figures, from whom he hoped to elicit some encouragement and comments that would help boost sales. Matthew Arnold (1822–1888), Robert Browning (1812–1889), Algernon Swinburne and John Addington Symonds were all on his mailing list. To Robert Browning he gushed, *Will you accept from me the first copy of my poems – the only tribute I can offer you in return for the delight and the wonder which the strength and splendour of your work has given me from my boyhood.*[8] With the eccentric academic and prolific author Oscar Browning (1837–1923), he made no secret of the fact that he was angling for a review: *If you get the opportunity and would care for it, I wish you would review my first volume of poems just about to appear: books so often fall into stupid and illiterate hands that I am anxious to be really <u>criticised</u>: ignorant praise or ignorant blame is so insulting.*[9]

Ignorant blame was not long in coming. The Secretary of the Oxford Union, the debating society at which many future politicians have cut their teeth, wrote to Oscar asking if he would donate a copy of *Poems* to the Union Library. This he duly did, in October, but at a subsequent gathering at the Union, Oliver Elton, later a literary historian, rose to his feet to attack the book, declaring, 'it is not that these poems are thin – and they *are* thin: it is not that they are immoral – and they *are* immoral: it is not that they are this or that – and they *are* all this and all that: it is that they are for the most part not by their father at all, but by a number of better-known and more deservedly reputed authors. They are in fact by William Shakespeare, by Philip Sidney, by John Donne, by Lord Byron, by William Morris, by Algernon Swinburne, and by sixty more . . .'[10] This denunciation provoked uproar in the Union, and a successful motion (carried by a narrow margin) to have the book rejected. The Librarian was therefore put in the embarrassing position of having to send back a volume he had himself requested, with apologies. Oscar understood the delicacy of the Librarian's position, but was scornful of the Union members who had voted for its rejection: *My chief regret indeed being that there should be at Oxford such a large number of young men who are ready to accept their own ignorance as an index, and their own conceit as a criterion of any imaginative and beautiful work.*[11] Despite his spirited defence, the refusal stung.

Sadly for Oscar's self-esteem and literary prospects, the professional critics were not impressed with his *Poems* either. The *Athenaeum*'s anonymous reviewer decried the 'over-indulgence in metaphor, in affected neologisms, and in conceits behind which sense and reason are obscured,'[12], while *Punch* opined that the work was 'Swinburne with water', adding insult to injury by suggesting that the poetry was not even as daring as its author intended: 'The poet is Wilde/ But his poetry's tame.'[13] Even Oscar Browning, trying to be kind, urged readers to be 'charitable and patient'. The reaction in the United States was just as bad. Symptomatic of the puritanical society then dominant on the East Coast, the *Woman's Journal* in Boston declared pompously that no man should read these poems out loud in the presence of women; to rub in the point, the review was headed 'Unmanly Manhood'.

The appearance of *Poems* also had an unfortunate and unforeseen consequence. Frank Miles's clergyman father read them and was appalled, so much so that he cut out the page with the one he considered the most unhealthy in theme – probably 'Charmides', which at one point refers to an imaginary coupling with a statue. Canon Miles wrote to both Frank and Oscar, demanding that they cease living together, as Oscar was such an unhealthy influence. The irony was that Frank Miles was as least as perverse in his tastes as Oscar; not long before, after Frank had entertained a very young girl at home, Oscar had to keep the police at bay at the front door while Frank escaped out of a back window. But as Canon Miles told Oscar, 'you do not see the risk we see in a published poem that, which makes all who read it say to themselves, "this is outside the province of poetry . . . It is licentious and may do great harm to any soul that reads it."[14]

Oscar was thus obliged to find new lodgings at short notice, settling on rooms in Charles Street, off Grosvenor Square, where he could but reflect on his apparently shattered dreams and fortunes. His poems had failed critically. A proposed London staging of his play *Vera* came to nothing. He no longer had adequate surroundings in which to display his most prized possessions or to entertain Professional Beauties and other influential guests. Moreover, money was getting scarce. He had already disposed of most of his small inheritance in Ireland, and he was living well beyond his means. Fortunately, when his spirits were lowest, in melodramatic fashion a telegram arrived from Richard D'Oyly Carte, who was in New York, where *Patience* had opened in September. Sarah Bernhardt had apparently suggested to D'Oyly Carte that the public's interest in the comic opera would be enhanced if Oscar went over to America to give a series of readings, indeed to be a real-life Bunthorne, on show. Like a shot, Oscar cabled back: Yes. *If offer good.*[15]

It took a good couple of months to come to a final agreement, however, partly because the American public apparently wanted lectures, not readings, with a clear emphasis on what today would be called lifestyle. After much correspondence and reflection, it was decided that the title of Oscar's lecture would be 'The English Renaissance'. Aware that his oratorical powers did not match his conversational skills in more intimate situations, Oscar signed up for elocution lessons. He also designed and had run up a huge, fur-trimmed green overcoat, intended as much for effect as for keeping out the cold. His preparations and impending departure caused an extraordinary amount of comment in the British Press. The editor of *Truth*, Henry Labouchere (1831–1912), astutely recognised that Oscar had managed to turn himself into a celebrity, and that even if much of the British public had not quite understood the importance of such creatures, America had. 'The Americans are far more curious than we are to gaze at all those whose names, for one cause or another, have become household words, and in this I think they are wiser than we are, for it is difficult to realise the personality of anyone, without having seen him. Mr Wilde – say what one may of him – has a distinct individuality, and, therefore, I should fancy that his lectures will attract many who will listen and look.'[16]

Oscar's fashionability – particularly his taste for black silk stockings – attracted much attention in the United States

When the transatlantic liner *Arizona* pulled into New York late on 2 January 1882, the American Press came out on a launch to welcome him. Nonplussed by some of their questions, such as what he had thought of the crossing, Oscar was astonished later to see a newspaper headline: 'Mr Wilde Disappointed with the Atlantic'. Teasingly, a letter then appeared in *Truth*, saying 'I am disappointed in Mr Wilde', and signed 'The Atlantic Ocean'. The passengers were not able to disembark until the following morning, by which time Oscar had composed himself sufficiently to be able reportedly to respond to the customs officer's standard question whether he had anything to declare, *I have nothing to declare except my genius.*[17]

For several days he enjoyed a whirl of engagements with New York's High Society, as the darling, or at least the curiosity, of the moment. He had scores of letters of introduction to literary people and society hostesses, and one invitation often led to another. This gave Oscar little time to polish his lecture, as he should have done, though he did make enquiries about getting his play *Vera* staged in New York, and took the precaution of having it copyrighted, to protect against possible piracy. He first took to the stage himself on 9 January, at Chickering Hall in New York, where his lecture was a sell-out. His appearance met the audience's expectations, as he had put on the knee breeches that were part of the ritualistic costume of his Oxford Masonic lodge, though many spectators assumed this to be court dress. His coat was lined with lavender satin, and he wore black silk stockings, which provoked considerable comment. In contrast, his lecture was sober, even sombre, though at times challenging, as it articulated some of the basic tenets of the growing Aesthetic Movement. He was proclaiming the existence of an English Renaissance, whose effects, he argued, would be as profound as those of the Italian Renaissance. *To disagree with three fourths of the British public on all points is one of the first points of sanity*, he declared. Pre-Raphaelite creations were more real than the living, he maintained. Art conferred upon life a value it had previously lacked. In ringing conclusion, he pronounced that: *We spend our days looking for the secret of Life. Well, the secret of Life is Art!*[18]

For the next 10 months, Oscar criss-crossed North America, lecturing in most of the major

Oscar Wilde in his famous fur-lined coat during his American tour

cities, as well as far smaller towns such as Aurora and Joliet, Illinois. It was a gruelling schedule, which inevitably took its toll, though there were moments of diversion, such as in Boston, where 60 Harvard students turned up at one of his lectures, all attired in a caricature of aesthetic dress and bearing sunflowers aloft. The most enjoyable parts of the tour were the opportunities to meet a wide range of American literary figures, from Henry James (1843–1916) to Henry Longfellow (1807–1882).

In particular, Oscar was thrilled on 18 January to visit the sexagenarian poet Walt Whitman (1819–1901), who had been a hero of his ever since Speranza had read to him as a child verses from Whitman's *Leaves of Grass*. Whitman's health was far from good at this period and he was living with one of his brothers in Camden, New Jersey. He was charmed when Oscar arrived and declared with the solemnity due to someone visiting a literary master: *I come as a poet to call upon a poet*. It is highly likely that Whitman had expected and desired only a brief courtesy call from Oscar, but they got on so well so quickly that he pulled a bottle of his sister-in-law's homemade elderberry wine from a cupboard, and settled down for a prolonged discussion. They were soon calling each other by their Christian names, and when the bottle was finished, Whitman suggested they move to his den, where they could be on 'thee and thou terms'. There the conversation turned from the purely literary – as well as gossip about

Walt Whitman (1819–1901), now seen as one of America's greatest men of letters, was an autodidact who left school at the age of 11. He learned to be a printer and became intoxicated with words and books. A fine ear for music helped him develop a distinctive poetic voice when he started writing verses seriously in his thirties. There was also a large element of religious inspiration. He knew the Bible intimately and dreamed of a world in which all men would be united in ties of friendship. Pure as this sounds, there was also a strong homosexual undertone to his thinking.

mutual friends and acquaintances such as Swinburne – to the more sensual theme of beauty. For Oscar, the conversation made him feel as if he were in ancient Athens, which left him quite emotional. As he told a newspaper reporter afterwards, Whitman was *the grandest man I have ever seen, the simplest, most natural, and strongest character I have ever met in my life . . . the closest approach to the Greek we have yet had in modern times.*[19] When he returned to see Whitman in May, the old man kissed him on the lips, sealing the bond they felt between them.

Meanwhile, the lionising Oscar was receiving from certain sections of American Society and the public seems to have started to go to his head. In what was more than mere bravado or a pose, he gravely informed another of the countless journalists who came to see him, *I'm a very ambitious young man. I want to do everything in the world. I cannot conceive of anything that I do not want to do. I want to write a great deal more poetry. I want to study painting more than I've been able to. I want to write a great many more plays, and I want to make this artistic movement the basis for a new civilisation.*[20]

Such self-confidence for someone still relatively young inevitably struck some people as arrogance. Several of the famous men he met, including Henry James, were not favourably impressed. And Oscar began to find himself the butt of parody and mockery from some quarters, just as he had been in England. Some of this was playful, even affectionate teasing, such as the popular songs that started to appear, including 'The Flipitty Flop Young Man' and 'Oscar Dear', but other criticism was malicious. Oscar brushed the negative comments aside, though he did wonder aloud why Britons in America were treated so much worse than Americans in Britain.

As Oscar told Whitman, however, he felt great affinity for the American common man. Working class Americans had a directness that greatly appealed to him. Perhaps his most enduring memory of the long American tour was a visit he made to the mining town of Leadville, Colorado. As Oscar wrote to the actress Mrs Bernard Beere (whom he had interested in his play *Vera*), the audience at his lecture there was made up almost entirely of miners. *I spoke to them of the early Florentines, and they slept as though no crime had ever stained the ravines of their mountain home. I described to them the pictures of Botticelli, and the name, which seemed to them like a new drink, roused them from their dreams, but when I told them in my boyish eloquence of the 'secret of Botticelli', the strong men wept like children.*[21] Later Oscar was lowered down in a bucket into a mine, where he marvelled at the torsos of the men working down there. A new mineshaft was named after him as a celebration of his visit. Asked later whether he had not found the miners rough and ready, he retorted, *Ready, but not rough. They were polished and refined compared with the people I met in larger cities farther East.*[22]

Although Oscar's lecture tour ended in October, he decided to stay on in New York for another couple of months. This was partly for health reasons, as he had contracted malaria, but also so he could spend time in the city with Lillie Langtry, who had organised her own theatre company in England and was due to tour the United States. Armed with a huge bunch of lilies, Oscar met her off her ship and took her to see some of his favourite people, including the Canadian photographer Napoleon Sarony (1821–1896), who took iconic pictures of each of them. An even more important reason for lingering in New York

Sarony's 1882 portrait of Oscar Wilde has survived to become one of the most famous images of the writer

was that negotiations were proceeding slowly but surely for productions not only of his play *Vera*, but also of a new drama that he had been mulling over but had not yet written, *The Duchess of Padua*, a romantic melodrama, written in blank verse and set in 16th-century Italy, in which the eponymous anti-heroine murders her husband in the hope of being united with a lover, who is so shocked by her action that he tells her he hates her, prompting her to denounce him as the murderer.

An unavoidable result of staying on in America was that he spent a great deal of the money he had earned on his gruelling lecture tour. He would therefore return to England with a smaller nest egg than he had anticipated. But he could console himself with the fact that his American travels had boosted his reputation back home, at least amongst those who were favourably inclined. His movements and his utterances had been widely covered in the British Press, as Lady Wilde kept him informed. 'You are still the talk of London,' she wrote on 18 September. 'The cabmen ask me if I am anything to Oscar Wilde – the milkman has bought your picture! And in fact nothing seems celebrated in London but you. I think you will be mobbed when you come back by eager crowds and will be obliged to shelter in cabs.'[23] As Oscar spent New Year's Eve on board ship on the Atlantic, heading for home, he viewed the prospect with a mixture of exhilaration and trepidation.

A Far From Ideal Husband

*The charm of marriage is that it makes a life of
deception absolutely necessary for both parties.*

Oscar spent barely three weeks in England on his return from
America. It was as if the peripatetic lifestyle of the previous year
had made him unfit for domesticity, even the domesticity of
bachelorhood. He was able to come up with a more poetic explanation for his restlessness, arguing that he needed to find a place
conducive to writing his new play, *The Duchess of Padua*. Italy
ought to have been the obvious location, but he feared it might
be too expensive, and his spoken Italian was only a pale shadow of
his French. So he chose Paris.

Paris had the added attraction that the French literary scene
had a high reputation amongst British Aesthetes, as well as considerable notoriety amongst puritans, and not just because it was
the source of yellow-bound erotic novels banned in Britain.
Interesting things were happening there culturally, especially in
experimental verse and the theatre, which operated under far less
censorship than its English counterpart. Since the 1860s, the cafés
and literary salons of Paris had been noisy with often passionate
debate about the direction in which poetry should head. So-called
Parnassians, who acquired their name from the literary magazine
Parnasse contemporain, and included figures such as François
Coppée (1842–1908) and Sully Prudhomme (1839–1907), revolted
against the earlier Romantic poetic school and rallied to the

doctrine of Art for Art's sake, as elucidated by the poet and novelist Théophile Gautier (1811–1872). Though some of the Parnassians' philosophy naturally appealed to members of the British Aesthetic Movement, a certain rigidity of form was seen as a weakness. Paul Verlaine (1844–1896) – who had carried on a tempestuous relationship with the younger, brilliant Arthur Rimbaud (1854–1891) – acted as a kind of bridge between the Parnassians and the so-called Symbolists, such as Stéphane Mallarmé (1842–1898), who endeavoured to convey impressions by suggestion rather than realism or naturalism, and who favoured free verse forms. Conservative critics decried what they saw as the Symbolists' decadent morbidity, but that in itself was something to stimulate Oscar Wilde's curiosity. The little Symbolist writing he had read or heard about struck him as distinctly modern – always a very positive adjective in Oscar's vocabulary, despite his classical education. Indeed, Oscar believed that modern writers only existed in France. If he could conquer Paris in the way that some sycophants told him he had conquered America, then he would have something to crow about.

Oscar Wilde in Paris in 1884

He soon found an agreeable second floor suite at the Hôtel Voltaire, where he had stayed with his mother nine years previously. The sitting room became his workplace. He easily filled his evenings with social engagements, as several of his friends were living in or visiting Paris, and he had a sheaf of letters of introduction. Early on in his stay, at a dinner party, he was presented to a young expatriate British writer, Robert Sherard (1861–1943), who soon became a regular companion, although neither had taken to each other at first sight. Sherard (who had changed his name from Kennedy) was a great-grandson of the poet William Wordsworth (1770–1850), and had spent part of his childhood with his family in the same house as Victor Hugo (1802–1885), on the island of Guernsey. With such a background, it was perhaps not surprising that he craved a literary future for himself and admired creative talent.

Oscar proved to be far more interesting and profound than Sherard had been expecting, and Oscar was rather charmed by Sherard's puppy-dog qualities: young, blond, energetic, masculine, forthright and outspoken, though not especially bright. Despite the fact that Oscar once kissed him fully on the lips, Sherard never imagined there was anything sexual in Oscar's interest in him or other young men. They saw each other virtually daily during Oscar's stay. As they walked the streets, they would talk about literature and point out the sights to each other. Often their conversation veered towards marriage, which Sherard was then contemplating, but Oscar warned that marriage nearly always ends in betrayal or acrimony. He was in fact rehearsing some of the ideas, and maybe even some of the language, that he would use in his later comedies. Sherard was soon star-struck, and took to writing down Oscar's bon mots, including those he produced in French. In the evenings, they would often dine together in restaurants, as Oscar worked his way through the remains of his American earnings and an advance he had had from the American actress Mary Anderson (1859–1940) for the new play. Work on the *Duchess*, as Oscar referred to it, was proceeding well. He wore a white woollen dressing gown for its composition, and covered sheets of expensive paper with his distinctive scrawl.

The three-and-a-half months that Oscar spent in Paris also enabled him to make the transition to what he described as the 'second period' of his life. The Oscar of the second period, he told Sherard, *has nothing whatever in common with the gentleman who wore long hair and carried a sunflower down Piccadilly*.[24] As if to illustrate the point, Oscar took a Parisian hairdresser off to the Louvre, showed him a Roman bust – identified variously as Nero or Mark Antony – and got him to curl his hair in that style. Oscar was hungry for new artistic sensations and trends, which meant jettisoning a lot of what he had championed up until then. He would no longer pose as an Aesthete, wearing the increasingly hackneyed external symbols of his artistic persuasions, but would instead be more allusive in their promotion. *Punch*, which seems to have had its informants everywhere, trumpeted: 'To be sold, the whole Stock-in-Trade, Appliances, and Inventions of a Successful Aesthete who is retiring from business. This will include a large Stock of faded Lilies, dilapidated Sunflowers, and shabby Peacocks' Feathers, several long-haired Wigs, a collection of incomprehensible Poems and a number of impossible Pictures.'[25]

Oscar was able to send off the manuscript of *The Duchess of Padua* to Mary Anderson in mid-March, only a fortnight overdue. *I have no hesitation in saying that it is the masterpiece of all my literary work, the* chef d'oeuvre *of my youth*, he informed her immodestly, though there was not yet much else of any worth to compare it with. Oscar explained to Mary Anderson that the play showed passion as a kind of daemonic possession for which the possessed may ask and receive mercy. Such spin was to no avail; after a long, ominous silence, Oscar heard from her at the end of April that she had turned it down, on the grounds that it would seem hopelessly old-fashioned, writing cuttingly, 'The play in its present form, I fear, would no more please the public of today than would "Venice Preserv'd" or "Lucretia Borgia" [historical dramas of intrigue in Italian settings, by Thomas Otway and Victor Hugo respectively].'[26] The rejection was a bitter blow, made worse by the fact that no more money would be coming from that quarter. At least plans were going ahead to stage *Vera* in America in the summer.

Being in Paris made Oscar realise that he needed to understand and absorb the many important new movements in both literature and art if he was going to refashion himself. He began to familiarise himself with the work of Impressionist painters, such as Claude Monet and Camille Pissarro, and he attended the theatre regularly – on at least one occasion visiting Sarah Bernhardt backstage. He read many of the latest novels and poems. Some of these were the product of what would develop into *fin-de-siècle* decadence. Previously unspoken subjects were being aired publicly, and several writers, including Paul Verlaine, were addressing homosexual emotions. Oscar went to see Verlaine, but thought him very shabby and unimpressive. A brief meeting with Victor Hugo was even more disappointing, as the old man sat fast asleep in his chair. More spirited was the novelist and diarist Edmond de Goncourt (1820–1896), whom Oscar met twice. Oscar was quite a fan of the work Edmond and his late brother Jules (1830–1870) had done and de Goncourt savoured some of Oscar's anecdotes of America. But there was something rather repellent about Oscar, de Goncourt thought. He also noted in his diary that his visitor was 'of doubtful sex'.

Back in England, where Oscar reinstalled himself in mid-May, there was also some speculation about Oscar's sexuality. *Punch* had even gone so far as to describe him as a 'Mary-Ann', an unflattering and rather dated term for an effeminate homosexual. That in itself might have been cause to make Oscar think about marriage, to quash the rumours. But he was also coming under pressure from his mother, who was beginning to despair about ever getting Willie off her hands, so now turned her attention to Oscar's marital prospects. Both her sons, she declared frequently in their presence, ought to think seriously about finding an American heiress. It was very vexing that Oscar had failed to do

'I am engaged to Oscar Wilde and perfectly and insanely happy'

so during a whole year on the other side of the Atlantic. Such a union would solve not only his financial problems, but also, she secretly hoped, her own. But Oscar had no intention of making a marriage of convenience. He had known what it was like to love a woman, thanks to his experiences with Florence Balcombe, and it was not impossible that situation could be replicated.

Constance Lloyd was the granddaughter of a friend of Lady Wilde's, and was currently living with her grandfather and aunt in Lancaster Gate. A little over three years younger than Oscar, she was an attractive, talented young woman, with long, wavy chestnut-coloured hair and a good figure. Shy in company, she tended to avoid drawing attention to herself, but she was extremely well read and notably proficient in Italian as well as French. She also had determined and quite modern views, though she rarely ventured them in public. Oscar had been much taken with her on the few occasions when they had met prior to his departure for America, but it was only on his return from Paris that he suggested to his mother that she should invite Constance round to her house in Park Street, where Oscar was then staying. A courtship of a kind then developed, though Constance was not alone in being uncertain of Oscar's true intentions. He talked brilliantly, and knew how to amuse and flatter, but never quite turned the conversation in the direction of a relationship. When the two of them attended a meeting on the promotion of women's rights at the end of June – Constance's brother Otho playing what had now become his regular role as chaperone – Constance exclaimed in quiet exasperation, 'You know everybody says, Mr Wilde, that you do not really mean half of what you say.'[27]

Matters were put on hold in July, while Oscar delivered a series of public lectures on 'Personal Impressions of America' and 'The House Beautiful' in London and in various provincial towns and seaside resorts. The American talk was not surprisingly largely anecdotal, playing to a typical English audience's conflicting

Interior design burst into the consciousness of the enlightened middle classes during the second half of the 19th century. The 1868 book *Hints on Household Taste in Furniture, Upholstery and Other Details* by Charles Eastlake (1836–1906) represented a reasoned aesthetic backlash against the excesses of mid-Victorian décor, in which rooms had been crammed with symbols of the occupants' wealth, social standing and bourgeois taste. Edward Godwin, one of the key figures of the Aesthetic Movement, espoused the cause of simplicity and a minimum of ornamentation, drawing much of his inspiration from Japanese artefacts and aesthetic principles that started to attract attention in England in the mid-1870s.

feelings of envy and condescension towards their cousins on the other side of the Atlantic. But the lecture on 'The House Beautiful' caused Oscar far more work. He drew heavily on seminal books published on the subject by Charles Eastlake, as well as poaching ideas from Whistler and Edward Godwin.

At the beginning of August, he had to leave for the United States to attend rehearsals of his play *Vera*, which was due to open at the Union Square Theatre in New York on the 29th. The actress Marie Prescott had taken a strong liking to the play and it was thanks to her financial backing that it was being put on; she also played the title role. Oscar designed a red dress for her, made from vermilion cloth he had brought over especially from England; this was one of the few things about the production that really caused a stir. The audience on the opening night seemed to like the play well enough, but with a couple of notable exceptions, the critics were deeply unimpressed. Then as now, the *New York Time*s could make or break a play, and its verdict was damning. Oscar Wilde was 'very much a charlatan and wholly an amateur', an editorial declared, while denouncing the play itself as valueless.[28] Advance bookings dropped sharply. Marie Prescott's efforts to try to persuade Oscar himself to come on stage after each performance, as a sort of music hall turn, in the hope that this would attract new custom, got a dusty answer from him. So the play closed after just one week, though Miss Prescott did occasionally revive it on tour. Oscar went to Newport and Saratoga for a holiday, to lick his wounds, knowing full well the pleasure some of his rivals and enemies would have in gloating over his failure when he got back to London.

At least there was Constance to console him, though rather unfairly he presented her with a copy of *Vera* when he returned to England, and asked her what she thought of it. In what must have been an excruciatingly difficult note for her to write, she replied that she liked 'the passages on liberty and the impassioned parts, but I fancy some of the minor parts of the dialogue strike me as slightly halting or strained. I am speaking however only from aesthetic impressions and not from knowledge, so please don't let any remarks of mine weigh upon your mind.'[29]

If this was some sort of test, Constance passed it, because a fortnight later, Oscar proposed to her, at a time when both of them, by coincidence, were in Dublin. Having been jilted by an earlier fiancé, Constance had been reluctant to give her emotions free rein, but now that the strange but brilliant Mr Wilde had actually popped the question, she dropped her defences and was ecstatic. As she wrote to her brother Otho, 'I am engaged to Oscar Wilde and perfectly and insanely happy.'[30] If Oscar wrote similarly enthusiastically to any of his relations, none of the letters survive. It was the second half of January before he sent a letter to Lillie Langtry, informing her that *I am going to be married to a beautiful young girl called Constance Lloyd, a grave, slight, violet-eyed little Artemis with great coils of heavy brown hair which make her flower-like head drop like a flower, and wonderful ivory hands which draw music from the piano so sweet that the birds stop singing to listen to her.*[31]

Both families were quite pleased, and not a little surprised, by the match. The wedding had to be delayed for several months because Oscar had a whole series of speaking engagements up and down the country to honour. But, as Constance's Grandfather Lloyd discovered to his concern, the money Oscar was earning from doing this was only going to clear off a small portion of his accumulated debts. With no capital worth speaking of, and distinctly poor prospects, Oscar was hardly a great catch. Constance did have a small income of her own, which would rise to a respectable £900 a year when old Mr Lloyd died. Conveniently, he did just that, not long after the wedding. The ceremony itself went smoothly on 29 May 1884 (the bride and bridesmaids wearing dresses designed by Oscar) and the new Mr and Mrs Oscar Wilde were able to commission work on a house in Tite Street, which Oscar had already decided should be a model House Beautiful. He asked Whistler if he would take over responsibility for designing the interior, but Whistler declined, recommending Edward Godwin instead – a perfect, but expensive, choice. Problems with builders meant that it was not ready for occupancy until January 1885.

In the meantime, Paris was the natural destination for the honeymooners, who occupied a three-roomed suite in the Hôtel Wagram. Constance may well have been a little surprised when Robert Sherard turned up on the second day. Oscar went out for a walk with him leaving his new wife behind – setting a pattern she would have to get used to. Oscar regaled Sherard with the

Oscar's obsession with the interior design of his house on Tite Street in Chelsea turned it into the model for the Aesthetic movement

joys of deflowering a virgin wife on one's wedding night, to the young man's protestations; what Sherard probably did not realise was that it was a huge relief for Oscar to find that he actually could perform with a woman, as occasional attempts with prostitutes in previous years had not been very reassuring. Moreover, Oscar really did love Constance, even if it was a form of idealised love that sometimes came into collision with reality. Constance, for her part, at least for a while, looked on her husband as some kind of god.

Oscar took Constance to several exhibitions and to the theatre in Paris, notably to see Sarah Bernhardt in Shakespeare's *Macbeth*. But he also brought a large pile of books with him on his honeymoon and acquired even more while he was in Paris. In particular, he picked up a copy of the recently published novel *A Rebours (Against Nature)*, by Joris-Karl Huysmans (1848–1907) – a book later described by the critic Arthur Symons as 'a breviary of the Decadents'. Although Huysmans would later

The 'Divine' Sarah Bernhardt (1844–1923) was widely acknowledged on both sides of the Channel as the greatest tragedy actress alive. Her first major success came as Cordelia in *King Lear*, in a production at the Odéon in Paris and she sealed her reputation with roles such as Phèdre in Racine's eponymous play and Dona Sol in Victor Hugo's *Hernani*, both at the Comédie Française. When she went over to England in 1879, to play a season at the Gaiety, her 'golden voice' and emotional power brought her flocks of admirers. Her versatility ensured that she could successfully carry off any role, even after she had a leg amputated.

reject decadence for Christian morality, the book is an astonishing catalogue of sexual and sensual self-indulgence, as its aristocratic anti-hero, Duc Jean des Esseintes, turns his back on the real world in order to experiment with sensations. He surrounds himself with works of art that would 'point out the way to new possibilities and shake up his nervous system by means of erudite fancies, complicated nightmares and suave, sinister visions.' One of Des Esseintes sexual experiments is with another male. Reading the book, which he did hungrily, Oscar certainly had his nervous system severely shaken. It was if he were being shown a whole new dimension of life. The book's sumptuous enumeration of jewels, flowers and other physical manifestations of beauty, alongside sexual experimentation, had a profound effect on his artistic and psychological sensibility. The novel also brought to his attention the symbolic importance of the biblical figure of Salome (described in the book as she is portrayed in Gustave Moreau's colourful but sinister paintings), who would become something of an obsession.

Despite this sensual intervention into the opening stages of Oscar's marriage, his relations with Constance had a degree of normality, in that she found out in September that she was pregnant. The Wildes had returned to London earlier in the summer, but had had to move from lodging to lodging while they waited for the Tite Street house to be ready. Pregnancy put paid to hopes that Constance had of getting a job – a remarkably liberated ambition for a newly married woman of her time, motivated largely by a desire to augment the family budget, but also, one suspects, because she realised that domestic life with Oscar might not be totally fulfilling.

Oscar had taken considerable care in choosing the mood of the rooms at 16 Tite Street, as well as their furnishings. He even chose many of Constance's clothes for her, so she would fit in with the overall effect. The library, on the ground floor of the four-storey house, as was the dining room, was Oscar's bolt hole, where he could retire to smoke cigarettes (which he did a great deal) or to have intimate conversations with friends. The room had gold walls and ceiling, rising above a high dado in dark blue. The theme was distinctly North African or Middle Eastern, with lanterns and hangings, an inlaid table, ottomans and a single divan. The window was covered to keep out natural light. Oscar also had a study on the top floor. On the first floor were the drawing rooms; the predominant colour in the larger, rear room was green; the ceiling boasted two gold dragons painted by Whistler. Constance and he had separate bedrooms on the second floor.

Planning the House Beautiful helped Oscar prepare two new lectures to take on tour in the provinces, on 'The Value of Art in Modern Life' and 'Dress'. He argued that fashion was the enemy of proper dress, *merely a form of ugliness so unbearable that we are compelled to alter it every six months*. He urged rebellion against bustles, corsets and stays, and all the other imprisoning and deforming accoutrements of ladies' apparel, declaring that garments should hang from the shoulders, not the waist, and should recall the simplicity of ancient Greece, or even ancient Britain. He took this message to the farthest corners of the country during an exhausting six-month schedule up to March 1885. And he wrote increasingly frequently about it in newspapers and magazines. Oscar got an entrée into journalism through his brother Willie, occasionally standing in for him when he was away, but soon he carved out an independent reputation for himself as an arbiter of taste, though many of his early articles were unsigned. He became a regular contributor to the influential evening newspaper, the *Pall Mall Gazette*, edited by the radical campaigning journalist, William Stead (1849–1912), amongst others. He also wrote numerous theatre reviews.

The Wilde's first son, Cyril – *an amazing boy*, Oscar crowed to his sister-in-law Nellie – was born on 5 June 1885. Oscar was thrilled to be a father, and Cyril would always remain

Constance with the Wilde's elder son Cyril, aged four, in 1889

his favourite child. Within a few months, Constance was pregnant again. But this time, maybe because he was in London much more, her ever more bloated body began to disgust him. One of the things he had always prized about her was her boyish figure – some friends even claimed she had a boyish face – whereas now she showed all the outward signs of womanhood. Far from being sympathetic to her condition, with its inevitable periods of sickness and languor, Oscar was often irritated, and preferred to be out of the house. Even the birth of his second son, Vyvyan, was no great cause for celebration, as he had rather been hoping for a girl; when Oscar finally got round to registering the baby, neither he nor Constance could remember precisely which day he had been born.

Moreover, Oscar had started to rediscover the pleasures of spending time away from his family, with intelligent, attractive young men. Harry Marillier was one such youth, an undergraduate at Peterhouse, Cambridge, who had known Oscar and Frank Miles at Salisbury Street when he was still a lad. Harry wrote to Oscar in November, to remind him of this and to invite him to Cambridge to watch him perform in an amateur play, which Oscar did. First, though, they met in London, where they had an intimate conversation – and maybe a cuddle or more – causing Oscar to write to the young man afterwards, *it was an hour intensely dramatic and psychological*.[32] Amongst the knowing, 'psychological' was often used during this period as a code word for male love. A few weeks later, Oscar wrote suggestively to Harry: *There is an unknown land full of strange flowers and subtle perfumes, a land of which it is joy of joys to dream, a land where all things are perfect and poisonous.*[33] This was a land Oscar was determined to explore.

It was while visiting Harry in Cambridge, paradoxically, that Oscar had the inspiration for the first of what would become a series of children's stories, collected in two volumes, *The Happy Prince* and *The House of Pomegranates*. This first tale, which recounts the tragic story of the love felt by a statue for a swallow, eschews the heavy-handed morality of many fairy stories of the period, while at the same time offering differing levels of understanding for children and adults. Over the next few years, Oscar enjoyed writing others that could be told to his own little boys, but which would carry more sophisticated messages to an adult readership, such as the pain of love, the nature of selfishness and the power of physical beauty.

In his own personal life, Oscar was increasingly drawn to the 'perfect and poisonous'. One day, while out shopping with Constance at Swan and Edgar's department store at Piccadilly Circus, his eyes caught those of a young male prostitute loitering outside. *Something clutched at my heart like ice*, he later recalled. He wanted the boy, and the boy knew it. This was not a desire that could be stifled.

Oscar was in fact very lucky that the first penetrative sexual experience he had with a boy was with someone healthy, intelligent, trustworthy and immensely precocious for his age. Robert Ross – usually called Robbie or Bobbie – was the 17-year-old scion of a distinguished Canadian Liberal family, who lived with his widowed mother in South Kensington. There is some dispute about how he and Oscar first met – the Irish writer and libidinous adventurer, Frank Harris wickedly spread the story that it was in a public lavatory – but what does seem clear is that the puck-like Robbie set out to seduce Oscar, and did not meet much resistance. Later, Oscar would look back in amusement at this revelatory experience, canonising Robbie as St Robert of Phillimore [Gardens], *Lover and Martyr – a saint known in Hagiographia for his extraordinary power, not in resisting, but in supplying temptation to others*.[34] Robbie had redeemed Oscar, at the age of 32, from the life of bourgeois respectability and sexual normality into which he had felt himself sinking. Moreover, when the physical side of the relationship with Robbie waned, a deep love remained, especially on Robbie's side.

It was a disastrous time for Oscar to be discovering and exploring his homosexuality. Though sodomy had long been a crime in England, other sexual relations between men were not, until the passing of the so-called Labouchere Amendment in 1885 outlawed acts of 'gross indecency' between males.

Overnight, hundreds of thousands of British men were turned into criminals, even if they had not engaged in anal sex. Since living in London, Oscar had started to develop a fascination for the criminal classes, whom he encountered on his expeditions to the poorer parts of the city, as well as seeing them loitering in the West End; now he could feel solidarity with them. Any further pursuit of homosexual activities would

Henry Du Pré 'Labby' Labouchere (1831–1912) was a journalist and Liberal MP who made a career out of exposing fraud, corruption and hypocrisy. London was awash with tens of thousands of prostitutes, many of them young girls. This led to moves to raise the age of consent for girls from 13 to 16, and to suppress brothels. During the committee stage of the relevant Bill, Henry Labouchere introduced an amendment designed to protect young boys as well, which effectively outlawed male homosexual acts. Labouchere had been one of Oscar Wilde's strongest supporters at the outset of Oscar's career, because of his iconoclastic satire, but the Labouchere amendment would be the instrument of his downfall.

again put him at risk of prosecution, but he felt instinctively that it was the law that was wrong, not same-sex love and intimacy. Several of London's male brothels, at least one of them staffed by off-duty telegraph boys, were closed down in the witch-hunt against homosexuals in the years following the passing of the Labouchere Amendment, and gay pick-up places came under greater surveillance, by both the police and potential blackmailers. Many of the patrons of such establishments decided that there were really only two sensible courses of action for them to take: either to go abroad, or to moderate their behaviour. Having just discovered the pleasurable reality of something he had presumably been thinking about for some time, Oscar was not inclined to surrender in the face of society's prejudices. But it was not only Oscar's developing sexuality that made him something of a natural outlaw. He also had sympathies for Irish nationalists challenging oppressive British rule, and for the desperate poor who sometimes chose illegal means to survive in a society in which there was no public welfare system.

Like so many gay and bisexual men in England, Oscar soon found himself leading a double life. At least for a while, he maintained quite a convincing façade as a happily married man with two children, who had put aside the flamboyant postures of his youth. Constance herself wanted to believe this was the case, and seems to have turned a blind eye to evidence to the contrary. She avoided speculating too deeply about what Oscar got up to outside the house, or even with friends and visitors inside it. This included Oscar's relationship with Robbie Ross who, astonishingly, moved in with the Wildes for several months in 1887, as a paying guest, while his mother travelled abroad. No record exists of how this arrangement came about, but it is possible that Robbie's mother and Constance knew each other from political or charity events, as Constance was an active member of the Chelsea Women's Liberal Association. The atmosphere at the dinner table must sometimes have been strange, as young Robbie and Oscar exchanged knowing glances, while upstairs the Wilde children were asleep in the nursery.

The money from Robbie's mother would have come in handy for the Wildes, though Oscar had by now succumbed to the necessity of taking a job. In April 1887, he accepted an offer from the publisher's Cassell to become editor of a monthly magazine called *Lady's World*, from the November issue. Typically, one of the first things he did when he took over, to assert his independent spirit, was to change the title to *Woman's World*. For several weeks after his appointment began formally, he travelled on the underground to Cassell's offices off Fleet Street, and assiduously solicited articles from possible contributors, including his own mother. The magazine published articles not only on dress and housekeeping, but also on feminism, women's suffrage and women's experiences in various professions. But as the months went by, he attended the office less and less. Despite the early burst of enthusiasm, his heart was not really in it, and the arrangement came to an end after two years.

Far more satisfactory was the three-part serialisation in May of his long story *Lord Arthur Savile's Crime,* in the *Court and Society Review*. Crime mysteries in the manner of Wilkie Collins and Edgar Allan Poe were popular at this time. But Oscar gives many new twists to the genre in his story, just as he had reshaped the fairy tale in *The Happy Prince*. The main story involves the dilemma facing Lord Savile, when a palm-reader predicts that he will murder someone. The suspense is handled well, but the tone is sometimes that of a black comedy. And there is a clear satirical dig at the then fashionable custom in London Society of chiromancy, even though Oscar was himself deeply superstitious and a believer in the power of genuine palmistry.

Oscar was getting increasingly concerned about what the future might hold. Marriage and fatherhood had lost their novelty, and he sensed that the relationship with Robbie Ross was not a real alternative. Robbie was going to go up to Cambridge the following year, and would carve out his own life and priorities, though he would always remain Oscar's most devoted friend. Even with his new responsibilities at *Woman's World*, Oscar was not exactly doing anything strikingly worthwhile. As a gossip column in the *Pall Mall Gazette* noted tartly, 'Oscar's star has been low on the horizon since he cut his hair and became "Benedick the married man" [the taunting epithet used against the witty Benedick in Shakespeare's *Much Ado About Nothing*].'[35]

The one saving grace was that he had completed enough children's stories to produce a book of them, *The Happy Prince and Other Tales*, which was published in May 1888. Oscar sent a copy to the Prime Minister, William Ewart Gladstone (1809–1898), who was an omnivorous reader, with the covering note, *It is only a collection of short stories, and is really meant for children, but I should like to have the pleasure of presenting it, such as it is, to one whom I, and all who have Celtic blood in their veins, must ever honour and revere, and to whom my country is so deeply indebted.*[36]

For once, Oscar the Irish word-spinner was under-selling himself. Most of the critics loved the book. Walter Pater praised the 'delicate touches and pure English' of the collection[37], while the *Athenaeum* went so far as to compare its author with Hans Christian Andersen. Maybe life was not quite so bad after all.

The Golden Boy

There is no such thing as a moral or an immoral book.
Books are well written or badly written. That is all.

For years, Oscar had put women on a pedestal, but marriage to Constance had brought them down to earth. Now he began to put young men on a pedestal instead, and he had a good idea of what his perfect type would be: not too tall, pale-skinned, probably blond (or *golden-haired*, as Oscar would have it) and beautiful; ideally an Oxbridge undergraduate, or at least someone with the intellectual capacity to be able to discuss art as well as life; and preferably a good listener, to act as a sounding-board for Oscar's own ideas, as well as being a potential acolyte. He took to visiting Oxford regularly, as it was fertile ground for meeting likely candidates, and he could always use the excuse that he was revisiting his alma mater.

He could find many historical precedents for championing the idea of a relationship between an educated man of experience and a beautiful youth on the threshold of life: his classical education had not been for nothing. But could one justify or extol it from within the British, and more specifically, the English tradition? One way, of course, was to bring the greatest of all English writers, William Shakespeare, into the argument. Today, given all the academic speculation about the true identity of the addressee of some of Shakespeare's sonnets, this appears a not unreasonable proposition. But for most people in late 19th-century England, to maintain that Shakespeare was a boy-lover was a form of cultural blasphemy. Oscar was well aware of this, but it did not put him off writing a long story, which he entitled 'The Portrait of Mr W H'. The 'W H' in question was Will Hughes or Hews, a boy-actor who played girl's roles, with whom Shakespeare was in love, according to a theory propounded by one of the characters in the story, which skates a narrow line between fact and fiction. The story grew out of conversations Oscar had been having with Robbie Ross, very soon after they met. Oscar was already at work on it towards the end of 1887, though it was not published until 1889.

Several of Oscar's friends whom he talked to about the project, including the politicians Arthur Balfour (1848–1930) and Herbert Asquith (1852–1928), urged Oscar not to try to get the story published, arguing that it could corrupt public morals. Others warned him, correctly, that it would bring an unwelcome spotlight onto his own private life. But Robbie Ross and other friends were keen for Oscar to go ahead. He decided he would, though initially with a version in which the homoerotic element was watered down. Oscar visited his near neighbours, the painters Charles Ricketts and Charles Shannon (whom, because they lived at 1 The Vale, Oscar had dubbed 'The Ladies of the Vale') to try to persuade one of them to do an illustration for the story. Ricketts and Shannon were one of the few socially acceptable gay couples then living openly together in London, though this was the first time that Oscar had met them. They seem to have averted the wrath of the Law and Society by steering well clear of gay venues and avoiding the transgressive faux pas of associating with working-class youths. Ricketts agreed to do a drawing. Oscar had hoped that Frank Harris, then editing the *Fortnightly Review*, might accept the story for publication, but Harris happened to be abroad at the time and his assistant flatly rejected it.

Oscar had better luck with *Blackwood's Magazine*, which brought out the expurgated version of the story in July. As a story in a magazine, it was not widely reviewed, but what comments it received were basically hostile. Worse, folk now started talking behind Oscar's back. Frank Harris later claimed that it was from this moment on that some people hoped for Oscar's downfall. Oscar was very proud of the story, however, and the theme of the love between a man and a youth became his central intellectual concern for a while.

The one problem about any young man, he lamented, was that his youth would inevitably be evanescent. This was hardly an original realisation on Oscar's part, but it troubled him greatly. It was true that one could capture the beauty of a young man at his zenith by commissioning a painting. But even if the painting stayed as a memory, one would have the sad reality of the physical body aging and deteriorating. What a shame things could not be the other way round! This conceit was the genesis of Oscar's only novel, *The Picture of Dorian Gray*. Though flawed in its construction, *The Picture of Dorian Gray* was a seminal work, both for Oscar and for English literature. It says what had been unsayable, and in its best parts, sparkles with wit and epigrams, some of which form the headings of the chapters of this book. In fact, *Dorian Gray* is almost all dialogue, as Oscar himself recognised, lamenting that he was incapable of sustained descriptive prose. All three main characters – the narcissistic Dorian Gray, who makes a Faustian pact to preserve his youthful looks; the painter Basil Hallward, who ensures that Dorian's portrait is his masterpiece; and Lord Henry Wotton, the highly intelligent but world-weary cynic – are all

'You have a wonderfully beautiful face, Mr Gray. Don't frown. You have. And Beauty is a form of Genius – is higher, indeed, than Genius, as it needs no explanation. It is of the great facts of the world, like sunlight, or spring-time, or the reflection in dark waters of that silver shell we call the moon. It cannot be questioned. It has its divine right of sovereignty.' Lord Henry Wotton in *The Picture of Dorian Gray*

aspects of the author himself. Lord Henry Wotton gets most of the best lines, many of them from Oscar's accumulation of bons mots, and therefore seems the most obviously Wildean. But Hallward is a creative artist, like Oscar, and in a sense Dorian is his creation; Dorian is how Oscar would have liked to see himself in another age, not to mention another body. Significantly, Dorian is corrupted by reading a book, rather similar to Joris-Karl Huysmans's *A Rebours*, which had so bewitched Oscar on his honeymoon.

A first version of *The Portrait of Dorian Gray* was published in the July 1890 edition of the American publication, *Lippincott's Monthly Magazine*, whose editor's decision to take the risk of publishing something so controversial was vindicated when this issue of the magazine sold out; a somewhat revised text appeared in book form in England the following year. Much of the British Press reviewed it as soon as *Lippincott's* was available. They were unsparing with their invective. 'Why go grubbing in muck-heaps?' *The Daily Chronicle* asked. The *St James's Gazette* saw pernicious foreign influences at work: 'it is a tale spawned from the leprous literature of the French Decadents'. Uncharacteristically subdued, *Punch* argued that 'a truer art would have avoided both the glittering conceits, which bedeck the body of the story, and the unsavoury suggestiveness which lurks in its spirit.'[38]. The general consensus was that it was an immoral book, which gave people cause to wonder whether Oscar was immoral too.

Poor Constance complained that after Oscar wrote *Dorian Gray*, 'no one will speak to us', but this was not strictly true. Certainly, some of the Wildes' friends dropped them. But others saw the work as by far the best thing Oscar had written up till then. His mother was rhapsodic about it. Even more important, from Oscar's point of view, it brought him a new wave of youthful admirers, several of whom wrote to him or sought him out. These included the Oxford undergraduate and aspirant poet

Lionel Johnson (1867–1902), whom Oscar, despite the fact that he had already started an affair with another young poet John Gray (1866–1934), hurried off to meet. The surname of Oscar's new lover was no coincidence, as the two of them had met while Oscar was writing the book, and Oscar named the central character after him. Deeply flattered, John Gray started calling himself Dorian and thinking of himself as Oscar's consort.

For a while Oscar was enchanted with John Gray, who was an extremely handsome young man and had the added advantage of looking several years younger than his actual age, 24. His origins were humble. His father was a carpenter and he himself became a metal-turner when he had to leave school to earn some money at the age of 13. Already he had dreams of a better life, however, and he taught himself languages, art and music in his spare time. His studies paid off, as he managed to pass the civil service examinations three years later, going to work as a clerk first for the Post Office and then for the Foreign Office. He was fastidious about his dress, speech and manners, successfully obscuring his background. But he was frustrated by the fact that Oscar did not want to see as much of him as he would have liked. As Oscar was trying to balance writing, maintaining at least the semblance of a family life and discovering new young friends, it was not surprising that he did not have very much time to devote to the rather demanding John Gray. Moreover, although their relationship lasted at least two years, maybe more, Oscar began to tire of him, as he tired of most of the young men he became involved with – with one notable exception.

That exception was Lord Alfred Bruce Douglas (1870–1945), youngest son of the 9th Marquess of Queensberry, and a student at Oscar's old Oxford college, Magdalen. Lionel Johnson brought him to Tite Street to have tea with Oscar one afternoon in June 1891, after Lord Alfred insisted on meeting the author of *The Picture of Dorian Gray*, which he claimed to have read nine times over. Oscar was flattered by Lord Alfred's bubbling enthusiasm and was impressed by the young man's aristocratic good looks, his alabaster skin, golden hair and cornflower-blue eyes. Lord Alfred – or Bosie, as he was known to family and friends – did not find his host physically prepossessing. The socialite Lady Colin Campbell had described Oscar not unfairly as a 'great white caterpillar', while the young Max Beerbohm (1872–1956) caricatured him as 'an enormous dowager'. He was overweight, ungainly and had bad teeth. But Bosie was flattered that such a distinguished man should pay him so much attention. Oscar insisted on taking him out for a meal to the Lyric Club a few days later, where he made his sexual interest in the young man obvious and presented him with a copy of the recently issued large paper edition of *Dorian Gray*. According to Lord Alfred's memoirs, which cannot always be trusted, Oscar then bombarded him with letters, invitations and books, in effect laying siege to him. That was not quite how Oscar recalled things in his great prison epistle *De Profundis*. According to that, he was far too busy in the second half of 1891 to devote much time to anyone, even an attractive young Lord.

Indeed, Oscar had entered a period of great literary fertility. The previous winter he had published an important political essay, far more serious in content than anything in his output so far: *The Soul of Man under Socialism*, which appeared in *The Fortnightly Review*. Debates about the true nature of Socialism were raging at the time, with proponents such as

Lord Alfred Douglas, the gilded Bosie in 1891

the designer and poet William Morris (1834–1896) arguing that capitalism and industrial mass production had destroyed craftsmanship and human dignity, while the formerly ardent proponent of secularism and birth control, Annie Besant (1847–1933), pursued her socialist inclinations by turning to Theosophy and disappearing off to India. Such writers and thinkers foresaw a Utopian future, reached through political and social change. Oscar's essay was both serious and witty, picking up many of the ideas that Annie Besant had developed, but he saw socialism as a means, not an end. *Socialism will be of value simply because it will lead to individualism*, he asserted, thereby challenging one of the chief objections of the opponents of socialism that it would lead to conformity and subjugation. He argued that the problem with most people's existence was *the sordid necessity of living for others*. Now and then, writers like Keats or Gustave Flaubert, or the scientist Charles Darwin, had been able to isolate themselves, *out of reach of the clamorous claims of others*. Altruism spoils people's lives, but they are forced into it by being confronted with hideous poverty, ugliness and starvation. For some of Oscar's friends, it was hard to reconcile the extravagance of his personality and lifestyle with such seemingly serious social and political philosophy, even if some might have suspected that at least part of his rhetoric was tongue in cheek.

More significantly, Oscar's career as a playwright was beginning to take off. *The Duchess of Padua*, retitled *Guido Ferranti*, was at last staged in New York in January 1891, and Oscar had hopes that the actor-manager George Alexander (1858–1918) would put the play on, under its original title, in London. Instead, Alexander commissioned Oscar to write a modern play, paying him £50 in advance. It took Oscar several months to work out a plot, but by the summer the structure of *A Good Woman*, later retitled *Lady Windermere's Fan*, had begun to take shape. Oscar deliberately chose the format of a social comedy, as he hoped to emulate the commercial success of popular dramatists such as Arthur Wing Pinero

(1855–1934). Once he began writing, the dialogue flowed easily, so he was already able to read the completed play to Alexander in October. At the end of the reading, when Oscar asked Alexander if he liked it, Alexander replied that it was 'simply wonderful', and offered him £1000 for it. *A thousand pounds!* Oscar exclaimed. *I have so much confidence in your judgement, my dear Alec, that I cannot but refuse your generous offer – I will take a percentage.*[39] It was a shrewd move, which would net him more than he could have dreamt of. As his 37th birthday loomed, success was finally beckoning.

With an agreement signed for a production of *Lady Windermere's Fan* early in 1892, Oscar set off for Paris. He already had another project in mind, a play in French, which, he laughingly told friends in London, would guarantee his entry into the Académie Française. The theme that had imposed itself upon him ever since reading Huysmans' *A Rebours* was Salome, the daughter of Herod Philip and Herodias, at whose behest John the Baptist was beheaded, after she danced for her besotted stepfather and uncle, Herod Antipas, as referred to in the Gospels of Matthew and Mark. He was aware that his friend, the French Symbolist poet Stéphane Mallarmé was also trying to write a major work about the princess who demanded John the Baptist's head on a platter after he refused her advances, but it was something of a standing joke in Paris how long Mallarmé was taking over it. Oscar's pattern of work was far brisker, and he was more single-minded. Even when he was out walking with friends in the boulevards, his conversation fizzed with ideas about how the play might take shape. Already he was envisioning Sarah Bernhardt in the title role, dancing naked before the Tetrarch. In his rooms, he would write down snatches of text, then get young friends like the writers Marcel Schwob (1867–1905) and Pierre Louÿs (1870–1925) to correct his French.

It was through Pierre Louÿs that Oscar got to know the solemn 22-year-old poet and writer, André Gide (1869–1951). They had

Though no longer as popular as he used to be, for much of the 20th century André Gide (1869–1951) was considered to be the supreme French stylist. He was prolific in his output of novels, memoirs, diaries and poetry. He developed a passion for travel, especially in North Africa, where he had many adventures with Arab boys. These experiences enabled him to throw aside the oppressive Protestantism in which he had been brought up. In maturity, he won worldwide fame with morally challenging works such as *The Immoralist* and *The Vatican Cellars*, as well as several volumes of confessional autobiography and journals, for which he was awarded the Nobel Prize for Literature.

seen each other at a couple of parties towards the end of November, but at Gide's request, Louÿs organised a small dinner in a restaurant so he could observe Oscar more closely. Oscar and André then saw each other daily for the rest of Oscar's stay in Paris. Sometimes at meals Gide would sit silently staring at his plate, as if crushed by the force of Oscar's eloquence and the daringness of the subject matter, which seemed to challenge almost everything that Gide had learnt in his conventional and well-to-do upbringing. His moods fluctuated from exhilaration to despair, leading several of his friends to surmise that he had fallen in love with Oscar. Oscar was not in the least attracted physically to Gide, but the young man brought out his didactic side. When Oscar left, Gide had something approaching a nervous breakdown, and wrote to his friend, the poet Paul Valéry (1871–1945) that meeting Oscar was the worst thing that had ever happened to him.

For once mindful of the needs of his family, Oscar returned home to London in time for Christmas. But he found it impossible to concentrate properly at the house, with all the comings and goings and the noise of the children, so moved down to Torquay after a few days to finish *Salomé*. He was back in London again in time for the rehearsals of *Lady Windermere's Fan* in the New Year, though he found this such a stressful experience, because of disagreements with George Alexander over proposed changes to the plot, that he was exhausted by the time the opening night arrived.

The theatre was full on 20 February, when the curtain rose on the first of Oscar's four great comedies. Many of Oscar's friends and past and present admirers were in the audience, including Lillie Langtry, Florence Balcombe, Robbie Ross and a whole host of young men, many of whom, on Oscar's instructions, were wearing green carnations in their buttonholes. When someone asked Oscar what these meant, he claimed that they meant nothing, but would leave people wondering. However, many of the wearers of this unnatural flower saw it as a badge of the particular fraternity to which they all belonged.

During the intervals there was a buzz in the theatre bars that confirmed Oscar's and George Alexander's belief that the play would be a great hit. The sparkling dialogue combined with a somewhat melodramatic plot kept the audience enthralled, and there was thunderous applause at the end. Responding to the calls of 'Author! Author!' Oscar wandered nonchalantly onto the stage, smoking a cigarette. He, too, sported a green carnation in his buttonhole. Then he gave what he described later as a *delightful and immortal speech*, declaring, *Ladies and Gentlemen: I have enjoyed this evening immensely. The actors have given us a charming rendering of a delightful play, and your appreciation has been most intelligent. I congratulate you on the great success of your performance, which persuades me to think that you think almost as highly of the play as I do myself.* Some critics in the audience considered this show of insolent bravado distasteful, but most of the audience were in a good enough mood to treat it as all part of the fun. Similarly, there was carping from some critics that the plot was flimsy and incredible, but as one of their number, A P Walkley, wrote: 'My answer is, "I know all that; but the great thing is that the play never bores me; and when a dramatist gives me such a perpetual flow of brilliant talk as Mr Wilde gives, I am willing to forgive him all the sins in the dramatic Decalogue, and the rest."'[40]

Constance Wilde had been in the audience, but slipped home quietly after the performance, also apparently willing to forgive her brilliant husband his sins. He stayed carousing with his young friends for a while, before retiring to the Albemarle Hotel, where he took his latest fancy, a young publisher's clerk named Edward Shelley, to bed with him for the night. It was a risky thing to do, but he was on the crest of a wave. And as the play ran on and on for months, pulling in glittering audiences, Oscar began to feel he was omnipotent.

In Oxford, meanwhile, Lord Alfred Douglas was leading an even riskier existence. He had been an enthusiastic participant in schoolboy homosexual antics while at his public school, and maintained his interest in teenage boys while at university. He particularly enjoyed encounters with working class boys, some of whom were 'renters', who slept with gentlemen for money. Bosie had no qualms about paying for sex, and sometimes he would give lads cast-off clothes and other presents. Considering he was partaking in highly illegal activities, the young Lord was remarkably careless. It was if he felt that as an aristocrat, favoured with good looks and a doting mother, he was somehow above the Law.

In the spring of 1892, while Oscar was still basking in the success of his play, he received an urgent appeal for help from Bosie, who was being blackmailed over an indiscreet letter. Though Oscar had had little contact with Bosie since the previous autumn, he sprang to his rescue, despatching his solicitor, George Lewis, to pay off the blackmailer with the princely sum of £100.

Bosie repaid Oscar's kindness in the only way he could, abandoning his practice of only going to bed with youths younger than himself by letting Oscar make love to him. Though Oscar was still involved with John Gray, and less seriously with Edward Shelley, he started to transfer his affections to Bosie. By the early summer, he had fallen in love. To Robbie Ross, who had now taken on the role of confidant, Oscar wrote from the Royal Palace

Hotel in Kensington: *Bosie has insisted on stopping here for sandwiches. He is quite like a narcissus – so white and gold . . . Bosie is so tired: he lies like a hyacinth on the sofa, and I worship him.*[41]

When Bosie was in good humour, he could indeed be charming and loveable. But he was a young man of violent moods. His mother, Lady Queensberry – who was divorced from his father – believed he had inherited his fiery temper from his Douglas forebears, some of whom had clearly been mad. A possible explanation for Bosie's mood swings and the way he would turn viciously against many of the people nearest to him, was that he suffered from paranoid schizophrenia or some similar mental condition of a type that was not recognised or understood when he was a young man. Many years later, his own son would be hospitalised with schizophrenia. The way some schizophrenics can work themselves into the lives and affections of people they target, only to set out to destroy them later, has an uncanny resonance with the affair between Oscar and Bosie.

Nonetheless, there seems little doubt that Bosie grew to love Oscar. He respected Oscar's literary talents and valued his advice. But he also increasingly depended on him financially. Thanks to the success of *Lady Windermere's Fan*, Oscar was well in funds, but when with Bosie, he lost all self-control when spending money. Bosie positively incited him to do so, exercising his power over the increasingly besotted older man to live a life of unnecessary extravagance. As Bosie later confessed to Robbie Ross, when Oscar was in prison, 'I remember very well the sweetness of asking Oscar for money. It was a sweet humiliation and exquisite pleasure to both of us.'[42] Bosie rooted out Oscar's latent masochistic tendencies, and exploited them ruthlessly. Yet there were times of great happiness together, which explains why Oscar was able to spend so much of the 18 months up to the end of 1893 in Bosie's company. There were frequent rows, which Oscar found almost unbearable, but there were also sweet reconciliations.

Their relationship did not exclude other adventures. On the contrary, Bosie encouraged Oscar to savour the wide variety of youthful possibilities available in London. Through a former public school boy called Alfred Taylor, who was the heir of a cocoa manufacturer, Wilde entered the world of male brothels and arranged liaisons with working class lads, several of whom he showered with gifts of cigarette cases and other mementoes. He would invite the boys to smart restaurants like Kettners, where one could hire a small private room, and later spend the night with them in hotels. Oscar even took one of his favourite boys, Sydney Mavor, to Paris with him for the French publication of *Salomé*. Plans for a London production of the play, with Sarah Bernhardt lined up to play the lead, had fallen through when the Lord Chamberlain's office refused it permission because of its depiction of biblical characters on stage. Oscar was so outraged that he threatened publicly to emigrate to France and change his nationality, causing much hilarity in the British Press.

He was a popular client with the rent boys of both London and Paris, not just because he was generous, but also because he treated them with courtesy and entertained them with funny stories. Bosie and he would swap notes about the boys they had bedded, and often they swapped the boys as well, as the physical side to their own relationship wilted and died, to be supplanted by an intense emo-

Sir John Sholto Douglas, Marquess of Queensberry (1844–1900) is remembered for two things: supervising the formulation of the Queensberry rules for boxing, and for getting Oscar Wilde sent to prison. A complex man with a violent temper, he was a keen cyclist and sportsman, but he also had an artistic side, writing not particularly good poetry. He rubbished the Christian faith, to the indignation of fellow Scottish peers, who ensured that he would not be amongst those chosen to represent them in the House of Lords. Although he claimed to love his three sons, he succeeded in alienating all of them, none more so than Lord Alfred.

tional bond. Neither of them made any attempt to conceal their love affair from their friends and they flaunted it in public. Oscar was for a while proud to do so, as he saw this as a defiant challenge to the narrow-minded morality of England, so different, he maintained, from the more open society in France. But gradually it dawned on him that Bosie's motivation for parading their relationship was different, as Bosie was determined to use it as a stick with which to beat his hated father, the Marquess of Queensberry.

Bosie could not forgive Queensberry for the way he had treated Bosie's mother and he despised many of the things that his father stood for. Amongst his other faults, Queensberry was an obsessive homophobe, who became convinced, probably rightly, that his eldest son Viscount Drumlanrig was having an affair with the Foreign Secretary and future Prime Minister, Lord Rosebery (1847–1929). He even tried, unsuccessfully, to get Edward, Prince of Wales, to take Rosebery to task over the supposed liaison. When rumours started to reach Queensberry that Bosie was involved with Oscar Wilde, he became convinced that his family was under siege from 'buggers'.

For the time being, though, Queensberry was not Oscar and Bosie's major worry. Bosie had foolishly given a spare jacket to one of his pick-ups, a 17-year-old lad called Alfred Wood, without checking if there was anything in the pockets. When the young man went through them, he found several letters from Oscar, including one that was deeply compromising and therefore perfect material for blackmail. In part it read, *My Own Boy, Your sonnet {'In Sarum Close'} is quite lovely, and it is a marvel that those red rose-leaf lips of yours should have been made no less for music of song than for madness of kisses. Your slim gilt soul walks between passion and poetry. I know Hyacinthus, whom Apollo loved so madly, was you in Greek days.*[43]

Alfred Wood dreamt of emigrating to America, where his prospects might be brighter, and he believed that the letter he had found would be worth at least enough to pay his passage. Not knowing how to contact Oscar directly, or maybe hoping to raise the stakes in his blackmail plan, he sent a copy of the compromising letter to the actor-manager Herbert Beerbohm Tree (1853–1917) at the Haymarket Theatre in the West End, where Oscar's second social comedy, *A Woman of No Importance*, was in rehearsal. Then he waited outside the theatre for Oscar to emerge. Tree forewarned Oscar, so when he confronted Alfred Wood and the boy claimed he could sell the letter for £60, Oscar nonchalantly informed him that he had never received such a princely sum for so short a composition, and he should go ahead and sell it. Non-plussed, the boy went away. But later he and two cohorts turned up at 16 Tite Street. This was an alarming development, but Oscar remained outwardly calm. Eventually, the young men handed over the bunch of letters saying that it was clear that Oscar was unwilling to be blackmailed and that he was also a kind man. As if to prove the second point, Oscar gave Wood £25 for his fare, and the boy duly left for America. Only later did Oscar realise that the most sensitive letter was not among the bunch that had been returned.

As a precaution against any further blackmail attempt, Oscar asked Pierre Louÿs in Paris to translate the text of the letter into French, portraying it as a poem in prose, in the hope that it could then be argued that it was merely a work of art. This Louÿs did, and the result was published in the Oxford undergraduate magazine *The Spirit Lamp*, which Bosie edited. But when Louÿs came over to London for the premiere of *A Woman of No Importance* on 19 April, he was shocked by what he saw of Oscar's behaviour. As the future author of several heterosexual erotic tomes, Louÿs was far from being a prude. But he was sickened by an incident he witnessed at the Savoy Hotel. Oscar and Bosie were sharing a suite there, in which there was one crumpled double bed, bearing testimony to the nature of their relationship. Constance arrived while Louÿs was in the room, bringing Oscar's post from Tite

Street. She begged Oscar to come back home with her. But Oscar joked callously that it was so long since he had been there that he had forgotten the address. Constance left in obvious distress. In her loneliness, she later turned in consolation to the bookseller Arthur Humphrys, with whom she developed a passionate friendship, possibly even a sexual affair. Louÿs reported what he had seen back to friends in Paris, and several of them decided to see less of Oscar, or even to break with him entirely.

Similarly, in London, Oscar's jilted lover John Gray was o bitter at being usurped that he cut off relations, and was taken up by the rich Russian dilettante André Raffalovich (1864–1934) instead. Others who dared criticise Bosie to Oscar could find themselves ostracised. Yet Oscar was himself sometimes driven to distraction by Bosie's temper and selfish behaviour. It was clear that this was the grand passion of his life, but as Oscar the scholar and artist was well aware, passion can end in tragedy.

The Lord of Life

It is perfectly monstrous the way people go about nowadays saying things against one behind one's back that are absolutely and entirely true.

Few other members of the audience at the opening night of *A Woman of No Importance* had Pierre Louÿs's insights into the playwright's psychology. But there were enough hints in the play for the more astute theatregoers to pick up some signs. The main plot is distinctly 'modern', in the sense that it flouted conventional Victorian morality: it transpires that the two main characters, George (Lord Illingworth) and Rachel (Mrs Arbuthnot, as she calls herself) when they had both just come of age had an illicit sexual relationship, which produced a son, but they then went their separate ways. Neither subsequently made any claim on each other; Mrs Arbuthnot actually turned down an offer of financial assistance from her lover's Mother. George and Rachel meet again, at a country house party in Norfolk, where their conversations are coldly rational. When Mrs Arbuthnot says that she has brought their son up to be a 'good man', Lord Illingworth retorts: *And what is the result? You have educated him to be your judge if ever he finds you out. And a bitter, an unjust judge he will be to you. Don't be deceived, Rachel. Children begin by loving their parents. After a time they judge them. Rarely, if ever, do they forgive them.* Even more daringly, in an early draft of the play, then titled *Mrs Arbuthnot*, the father is seen as having a homosexual interest in the son, without realising who he is. This element was toned down in the version as staged, in which Lord Illingworth merely offers the young man a job as his private secretary. But there was still enough that was shocking in the play for a few spectators to boo at the end, though most of the audience applauded enthusiastically.

The mixed reaction rather took the wind out of Oscar's sails, though he may also have had personal worries on his mind. As Max Beerbohm, who was present, recounted, 'When little Oscar came on to make his bow, there was a slight mingling of hoots and hisses, though he looked very sweet in a new white waistcoat and a large bunch of little lilies in his coat.'[44] Oscar uttered just one sentence: *Ladies and gentlemen, I regret to inform you that Mr Oscar Wilde is not in the house*. Max's half-brother, Herbert Beerbohm Tree, who had commissioned the play as well as acting in it, stepped forward gallantly and declared, 'I am proud to have been associated with this work of art.'

The Press was overwhelmingly positive. William Archer (1856–1924), a drama critic who had been one of the few to argue that *Salomé* ought to have been allowed on the London stage, judged that parts of the second act of *A Woman of No Importance* offered the 'most virile and intelligent piece of English play-writing of our day.' The *Times* was equally complimentary, declaring that 'The play is fresh in ideas and execution and is written moreover with a literary polish too rare on the English stage.'[45]

The second night audience was graced by the Prince of Wales and Mary Adelaide, Duchess of Teck, both of whom enjoyed it enormously and ensured that it would be talked about in high society. The play's success was guaranteed, mirroring that of *Lady Windermere's Fan*. So Oscar's spirits were in a more buoyant state when he went on from the theatre that evening to dine at the house of the American soprano Blanche Roosevelt. She had arranged for the celebrated French chiromancer Count Louis Hamon, alias 'Cheiro', to be present, and guests were invited to put their hands through a curtain so he could read their palms without being able to see who they were. In Oscar's case, Cheiro pronounced that the left hand, whose characteristics he said were determined by heredity, promised brilliant success, while the right, reflecting individual development, threatened ruin. When Oscar inquired when that ruin might occur, the palmist replied, 'At about your 40th year' – in other words, most probably in 1895. Oscar was deeply shaken by the reading, and left the house before the guests sat down to dinner.

Largely at Bosie's urging, Oscar decided to leave London in the late spring, renting a substantial house, inappropriately called 'The Cottage', at Goring-on-Thames. The house had lovely gardens and meadows that swept down to a towpath by the side of the river. There were eight servants to keep things running smoothly at The Cottage, and a boathouse from which guests could hire a variety of craft for their enjoyment. The idea was that Oscar would be able to get on with writing his next play, *An Ideal Husband*, in peace and quiet. But he was too gregarious to spend long periods on his own, so he invited various friends to come down to stay for short breaks, including his family and Harry Marillier, the former Cambridge undergraduate who had aroused Oscar's interest several years earlier. Cyril Wilde was now old enough to take an active interest in what was happening on the river and even to declare himself an infant supporter of Irish home rule. Bosie invited himself down to Goring whenever he felt like it, and, as always, demanded to be entertained when he got there. Once he turned up with a group of friends from Oxford, whom he felt did not get enough of a performance from Oscar, so he flew into a rage once they had left. Exhausted from such scenes, which prevented him from getting on with serious work, Oscar sighed: *We are spoiling each others' lives. You are absolutely ruining mine and evidently I am not making you really happy. An irrevocable parting, a complete separation, is the one wise philosophic thing to do*. Bosie duly departed after lunch, leaving one of his by now frequent poisonous notes behind. But within days he was asking to be forgiven, and Oscar, being weak, obliged.

Nonetheless, Oscar turned to Bosie's mother to discuss what could be done with her wayward son. Lady Queensberry was worried that Bosie would become a wastrel, but she was frightened of tackling him directly about this because of his temper. A sense of urgency was added to the matter when the young man left Oxford without a degree. He simply did not bother to sit the examinations, much to the irritation of the Magdalen College authorities. He probably would have done badly if he had, as he had spent hardly any time studying his supposed subject, Greats (Classics), even turning down Oscar's offer to tutor him. Instead, he preferred to write poetry, edit student publications and have fun. Oscar was dismayed, as going down without a degree would seriously damage Bosie's career prospects, but Bosie arrogantly proclaimed that as Percy Bysshe Shelley had managed perfectly well leaving Oxford without a degree, so could he.

Oscar decided to hatch a plot with Lady Queensberry to get Bosie out of the country. This would, they hoped, keep him out of trouble, while at the same time enabling Oscar to get on with his work. Lady Queensberry was a friend of Earl Cromer (1841–1917), the distinguished English colonial administrator who had since 1883 been Agent and Consul General in Egypt, a post he would hold for over 20 years. Oscar suggested that Bosie should go out to Cairo as an honorary attaché on Lord Cromer's staff, though he impressed upon Lady Queensberry that it was important that Bosie should not realise that the idea had initiated with him. In the event, there was no vacancy at the Consulate General, but Lord Cromer was generously willing to have the young man as a houseguest for a while.

This plan was subsequently brought into effect, though there were considerable difficulties and tantrums from Bosie before he was safely despatched. In the meantime, another of Oscar's bright ideas for his lover had gone disastrously wrong. Wanting to give Bosie something to do, he suggested that Bosie should translate his play *Salomé* into English. Such a job was worthy of Bosie's literary ambitions, Oscar argued, and it would mean that as the translator, Bosie would get his name on the title page of a proposed English-language book version of the play. Unfortunately, Bosie's French was nowhere near good enough for the task, and the manuscript he submitted to Oscar was full of schoolboy howlers. When Oscar remonstrated, Bosie flew into one of his rages, and said that it was not his French that was at fault, but Oscar's play. The young Francophile artist Aubrey Beardsley (1872–1898) then offered to get the English text into a publishable state, but his version was not considered adequate either. Beardsley recounted to Robbie Ross some of the details of the *Salomé* row, reporting with a certain degree of malicious pleasure, 'Bosie's name is not to turn up on the Title. The book will be out soon after Xmas. I have withdrawn three of the illustrations and supplied their places with three new ones (simply beautiful and quite irrelevant).'[46] The reason for the withdrawal of some of his drawings from the *Salomé* book was that they were considered too risqué. Some of them still have tremendous force today, including *The Dancer's Reward*, which shows Salome standing over the platter bearing Iokanaan's (John the Baptist's) head, holding it by the hair, blood pouring down on to the

Aubrey Beardsley (1872–1898) was a quintessential 1890s figure, who produced exquisitely executed black and white drawings of great individuality, discarding some of the Western norms of perspective and symmetry. He had a particular passion for grotesques and erotic figures, which often got him into trouble with publishers, not least because he had a habit of hiding shocking details in obscure corners of his finely-worked drawings in such a way that they were not always immediately visible. Plagued by ill health, he died of tuberculosis in the South of France at the age of 25.

floor. In more frivolous vein, Beardsley mischievously drew the moon, to which Salome often refers, as an unflattering caricature of a fat-faced Oscar.

With Bosie safely packed off to Egypt over the winter months, Oscar was able to concentrate on finishing *An Ideal Husband*. As he told several friends, the new play was something of a departure for him. While still rich in comic dialogue, the plot is far more serious, involving a politician who has achieved his position and wealth largely through selling a state secret when he was a young man. Elements of Oscar's own life and experience are visible in it, including attempted blackmail, as the politician, Sir Robert Chiltern, tries to avert exposure by a scheming lady of low reputation, Mrs Cheveley, who has stolen letters that she can use for extortion. The nice conceit of an 'ideal husband' being something of a criminal had a very Wildean moral message. As Oscar commented to Arthur Roberts, *The comic spirit is a necessity in life, as a purge to all human vanity.*[47]

Christmas 1893 was a rare period of domestic normality at 16 Tite Street. With Bosie safely out of the way, Oscar could relax with his family, taking particular joy in playing with the children. Financial pressures were considerably reduced with Bosie not around. As Oscar later recalled bitterly in *De Profundis*, an ordinary day's expenses with Bosie would easily run to £20 – a phenomenal sum for the period. Oscar's finances had got so bad earlier in the year that the local butcher refused to extend the Wildes further credit until their bill was settled – this despite the fact that Oscar was earning handsomely from his plays.

All was not well on the family front, either. Oscar refused to attend his brother Willie's second wedding in January 1894, relations with him having broken down completely. Willie's first marriage had been a short-lived union with a wealthy American lady who took him off to New York, where he showed no inclination to earn any form of living. He spent his days in a gentleman's club drinking, and doing cruel imitations of his younger brother, which inevitably got back to Oscar. Willie's wife declared after a short period that he was no use to her by day or night, and got rid of him. He was luckier with his second choice of bride, who made up for her lack of money by her sweet nature. Lady Wilde was distressed that Oscar could not bring himself to offer the hand of reconciliation to a brother whom he felt was a sponger who had helped spread unpleasant stories about him.

Oscar received many letters from Bosie while the young man was in Egypt, but he destroyed them after reading them and did not reply. He hoped that the separation could be made definitive, as he realised that the relationship could ruin his family in more senses than one, as well as hindering his writing. But Bosie was not one to give up so easily. His missives became ever more despairing, and after a long period of silence, he wrote to Constance instead, begging her to persuade her husband not to leave him without the prospect of meeting up again. Lady Queensberry for her part repeatedly urged Bosie to end his friend-ship with Oscar, saying it would do him no good. But he wrote back angrily in Oscar's defence, saying 'I don't believe I had a soul before I met him.' His mother accused Oscar of teaching him a peculiar view of morality, but Bosie countered with a paean of praise for Oscar's 'sunny nature, his buoyant "joie de vivre", his quick wit and splendid sense of humour, and his loyal kind and forgiving nature which make him altogether more like a grown-up boy than the sort of cynical subtle and morbid creature which you want to make him out.'[48]

Bosie was now going to test Oscar's forgiving nature to its limits. The Cromers had arranged for Bosie to go to Turkey to work as an honorary attaché with Lord Currie, the British Ambassador in Constantinople. Bosie made his way to Athens, where he showed no sign of hastening to his new post. Exasperated by this lack of diligence Currie withdrew his offer, and with a sigh of relief, Bosie headed for Paris, demanding that Oscar meet him there. Oscar telegraphed Bosie saying, *Time heals every wound but for many months to come I will neither write to you nor see you*. Bosie's entreaties became ever more extreme, hinting darkly at suicide. He knew Oscar's nature well enough to realise that he would never forgive himself for being responsible for the young man's death. Sure enough, Oscar relented, and went over to Paris to join him.

They travelled back to London together, where by chance the Marquess of Queensberry came across them lunching together at the Café Royal, one of Oscar's favourite haunts. They invited him to join them, and for an hour or so the Marquess was charmed by Oscar's wit and civility. But later that day, Queensberry had second thoughts, and wrote to his son expressly forbidding him to see Oscar, adding, gratuitously, that he had heard an (entirely false) rumour that Constance was petitioning to divorce Oscar on grounds that he had committed sodomy against her. Bosie responded with a simple seven word telegram that was bound to inflame his father's ire: 'What a funny little man you are.' Oscar was appalled when Bosie boasted about this, knowing that it would only goad Queensberry into more hostile action.

The two lovers took themselves off to the continent, in the hope of keeping out of Queensberry's way. They travelled separately, apparently believing that no one would realise they were together, but in Florence they ran into André Gide, who immediately communicated the fact back to Paris. Oscar soon realised it was impractical to stay away from London too long. He needed to be there to work, but he also now thought it would be wise to take legal advice in case Queensberry started to make trouble. Once back in London he therefore consulted George Lewis, only to discover to his dismay that Queensberry had already retained him. He therefore had to engage a solicitor recommended by Robbie Ross instead.

On 30 June, Queensberry turned up unannounced at Tite Street, accompanied by what looked like a hired thug, but was probably one of his boxing acquaintances. Queensberry accused Oscar to his face of corrupting his son. It was an unpleasant confrontation, made all the more intimidating by the presence of Queensberry's companion. At least it had not taken place in public, and after a while Oscar was able to get his two unwanted visitors to leave. Over the following weeks, Queensberry reportedly prowled between some of Oscar and Bosie's favourite restaurants and cafés, such as the Café Royal, Kettners and Willis's Rooms in King Street, hoping to catch them together so he could make a scene. This made life very difficult for Oscar, the self-styled 'King of Life', who until then had liked to treat the fine hotels and restaurants of London as an extension of his own drawing room.

To make matters worse, Bosie had acquired a gun, justifying this on the grounds of self-defence. Queensberry had written to him once that he would shoot Oscar if he found out that the impression they gave when they were together that they were having a homosexual relationship was true. Bosie's gun went off accidentally at The Berkeley one day, alarming Oscar as much as the rest of the clientele. This was one melodrama he did not wish to be part of. Moreover, he was starting to feel that he was being used by Bosie as a weapon in Bosie's own private war against his father. Yet he seemed powerless to withdraw.

Astonishingly, Oscar still managed to work. Financially, he had no other choice. Despite all the tension of his current predicament, he was at the peak of his literary powers. He had another play in mind, but before he settled down to that, there was a small piece of unfinished literary business dating from many years back. He had worked off and on at a long poem called *The Sphinx*; this he now finalised and brought out in a limited edition with the publishers Lane and Matthews, with a cover designed by Charles Ricketts. His wit undimmed, Oscar claimed, *My first idea was to*

Oscar Wilde's obsessive persecutor Lord Queensberry

print only three copies: one for myself, one for the British Museum, and one for Heaven. I had some doubts about the British Museum.[49]

In August, Oscar travelled with his family and a Swiss governess to Worthing. Finances did not stretch to anything as grand as The Cottage at Goring; in fact, the house they rented for a couple of months on the Esplanade at Worthing, called The Haven, was rather cramped. These conditions did not stop Oscar writing what would be his masterpiece: *The Importance of Being Earnest*. He already had a clear idea of what the play would be about, though he simplified the plot as the writing progressed. The basic point of the play, Oscar told Robbie Ross, only slightly tongue in cheek, was *that we should treat all trivial things very seriously, and all the serious things of life with sincere and studied triviality*. This comes over most clearly when one analyses the relative importance for several of the characters of love and marriage on the one hand, and whether one should have cake, cucumber sandwiches or buttered bread on the other.

JACK (*nervously*): Miss Fairfax, ever since I met you I have admired you more than any other girl . . . I have ever met . . . since I met you.

GWENDOLEN: Yes, I am quite well aware of the fact. And I often wish that in public, at any rate, you had been more demonstrative. For me you have always had an irresistible fascination. Even before I met you I was far from indifferent to you. (*JACK looks at her in amazement.*) We live, as I hope you know, Mr Worthing, in an age of ideals. The fact is constantly mentioned in the more expensive monthly magazines, and has reached the provincial pulpits, I am told; and my ideal has always been to love some one of the name of Ernest.

By early September, Oscar had enough of the play sketched out to be able to travel up to London to meet George Alexander over lunch at the Garrick Club and to extract a little money from him. Oscar was perpetually overdrawn at the bank, and there were some pressing bills to settle. He was safely back in Worthing, however, when his name was once more the focus of gossip in clubland

and in the press. The cause was the anonymous publication of a novel entitled *The Green Carnation*, which featured two preposterous characters, Esme Amarinth and Lord Reggie Hastings, who were only too clearly based on Oscar and Bosie. Though there is no overt suggestion of a homosexual relationship between the two characters, the young man is totally in thrall to his older mentor, who seems to be moulding him in his own image. Some people speculated that maybe

Oscar Wilde wearing the significant green carnation in his buttonhole, 1894

Oscar had written the book himself, as another bizarre form of self-publicity. Oscar wrote a letter to the editor of the *Pall Mall Gazette* disclaiming authorship: *I invented that magnificent flower. But with the middle class and mediocre book that usurps its strangely beautiful name I have, I need hardly say, nothing whatsoever to do. The flower is a work of art. The book is not.*[50]

In fact the novel was the work of a young man called Robert Hichens (1864–1950), whom Bosie had met in Egypt. Bosie, Hichens, the future novelist E F 'Dodo' Benson and a good friend of Oscar's, Reggie Turner, had all gone up the Nile on a tour together. Oscar was inevitably a frequent subject of their increasingly outrageous conversation, though none of the three others realised that Hichens was mentally noting a lot of what was being said. Some passages in the book – including Bosie's provocative telegram to his father – are taken word for word from real life.

A few years earlier, Oscar would probably have viewed the appearance of such a book as at best flattering, or at worst a minor nuisance. But he was aware how damaging it was now, when his relationship with Bosie was already the subject of tittle-tattle. Moreover, the way that in the book Lord Reggie sheepishly follows Mr Amarinth's aesthetic lead seemed to confirm the theory held by the Marquess of Queensberry and others that Oscar had led Bosie astray. This made Oscar's own position still more vulnerable.

By the time *The Green Carnation* came out, Constance and the boys had left Worthing, so when Oscar went out for a walk or to buy a newspaper, he was free to fraternise with some of the local boys whom he had met with Bosie when Bosie had come down on a short visit in the third week of August. Oscar became particularly fond of one 15-year-old lad called Alfonso Conway, and would often go out boating and fishing with him. According to Alfonso's later testimony in court, Oscar first made a sexual pass at him while out on an evening walk, after which the boy went several times to spend the night at The Haven. Before he left Worthing, Oscar took Alfonso on an outing to Brighton, where he bought him a suit, a pair of flannels and a straw hat.

Bosie came down to Worthing again in October, but soon announced that he was bored with the town and hated the house, so he insisted on moving to Brighton, where they booked into the Metropole Hotel (later incorrectly remembered by Oscar as the Grand). Unfortunately, Bosie then went down with influenza, and for the next five days, Oscar tenderly nursed him, reading to him and running errands. When Bosie had recovered, they moved into lodgings in the town, but this time it was Oscar who fell ill, presumably having caught the virus from Bosie. Bosie had no intention of playing Florence Nightingale, however, and went out into the town to enjoy himself, while Oscar was left to languish in bed, without even any water by his side. When he remonstrated with Bosie on the young man's return, Bosie flew into one of his tempers, even worse than any Oscar had witnessed before, then stormed off. It was Oscar's 40th birthday on 16 October, but instead of greetings

Oscar Wilde and Lord Alfred Douglas together in a studio portrait, 1894

or an apology, he received from Bosie a letter so poisonous that he could hardly bear to read it. It suggested that Bosie had been on the verge of attacking him when he was on his sickbed. And it concluded icily, 'When you are not on your pedestal, you are not interesting. The next time you are ill I will go away at once.'[51]

Oscar resolved there and then that Bosie was beyond hope and that there was no way he could continue seeing anyone so unkind, so amoral. He was quite firm in this resolve, until he was sitting on the train back to London on 19 October and opened up his newspaper, in which there was a report of the death of Bosie's older brother, Viscount Drumlanrig, apparently in a shooting accident. Later there was considerable private speculation that Drumlanrig may have committed suicide, possibly because of his alleged affair with Lord Rosebery, who had become Prime Minister in March. The Marquess of Queensberry had been hounding Rosebery, even travelling to Germany to try to confront him, just as he was now hounding Oscar. Whatever the truth of Drumlanrig's death, Oscar knew that Bosie would be devastated. All his good intentions of bringing their relationship to a definitive end were cast aside, and he telegraphed an affectionate message of condolence as soon as he reached London. The relationship was rekindled as if nothing untoward had happened.

While Bosie was embroiled in family matters following his brother's death, Oscar polished *The Importance of Being Earnest* and prepared himself for the opening of *An Ideal Husband*, which had its first night on 3 January 1895. The Prince of Wales was present, as well as several leading politicians. George Bernard Shaw (1856–1950) was among the critics who sang the play's praises, highlighting with approval the modern note in the hero's 'assertion of the individuality and courage of his wrongdoings as against the mechanical idealism of his stupidly good wife, and in his bitter criticism of a love that is only the reward of merit.'[52]

For once, Oscar did not surround himself with a coterie of exquisite young men at the opening night. Nor did he stay for the curtain call. But after the show, he and Bosie had dinner with Max Beerbohm and Herbert Beerbohm Tree at Oscar's club, the Albemarle. Oscar had reached a pinnacle few playwrights achieve, with one of his plays now on at a leading West End theatre, and another due to open in a matter of weeks.

Oscar would have liked to stay in London throughout January, to be present for the rehearsals of *The Importance of Being Earnest*, but Bosie had other ideas. As Oscar wrote to a relatively new friend, the novelist and satirist Ada Leverson (1862–1933): *I fly to Algiers with Bosie tomorrow. I begged him to let me stay to rehearse, but so beautiful is his nature that he declined at once.*[53] The ostensible reason for getting away was to escape the worst of the English winter. But the real motivation was that Bosie had heard from other travellers that Algeria was full of lovely, willing boys.

This did indeed prove to be the case. About a week after the couple's arrival in Algiers, Oscar was writing enthusiastically to Robbie Ross: *The Kabyle boys are quite lovely. At first we had some difficulty in procuring a proper civilised guide. But now it is all right, and Bosie and I have taken to haschish: it is quite exquisite: three puffs of smoke and then peace and love. Bosie wakes up at night and cries like a child for the best haschish.*[54]

From Algiers, they moved to the oasis of Blidah, where romantic trysts with what Oscar described as *fauns* could be made under the palm trees. More unexpected was the appearance of André Gide; Fate seemed to throw him and Oscar together. Gide was also anxious to get to know the local people better, though he was not yet as liberated sexually as Oscar and Bosie. When Bosie went off to Biskra in pursuit of a lad who had particularly taken his fancy, André and Oscar returned together to Algiers. There Oscar took André off to a café that he had discovered deep in the Casbah. André was puzzled to know the reason why, as it seemed such a gloomy, impoverished place, until a beautiful young musician arrived and started to play. André was startled when Oscar asked him outright *would you like the little musician?* André nervously said yes, and Oscar made the necessary arrangements. For Gide, it was one of the great turning points of his life.

André and Oscar spent several days in Algiers together, discussing literature and art, though when they had first bumped into each in Blidah, Oscar had announced, *I am running away from art. I want to worship only the sun.* He also shared his anxieties about what would happen when he returned to London. He was sure that the Marquess of Queensberry was plotting something, but he did not know what. Gide wondered whether Oscar would not do better to stay abroad, well out of the reach of Queensberry and of the preposterous British Law – a view that growing numbers of Oscar's friends would espouse. But Oscar said that was quite impossible. It was not just that he needed to be in London for the opening of his play. As he said to Gide, *It would mean going backwards. I must go as far as possible. I cannot go any further. Something must happen . . .*

De Profundis

One should never make one's debut with a scandal.
One should reserve that to give an interest to one's old age.

It was snowing heavily on the evening of 14 February, when *The Importance of Being Earnest* opened at the St James's Theatre. Being St Valentine's Day, many of the couples present among the audience were in a romantic mood and the light-hearted handling of the theme of courtship and marriage went down extremely well with the public. The play is a fast-moving farce, requiring skilful direction and acting to succeed; Oscar declared *it must be like a pistol shot.* The play deploys several of the characters and situations that were familiar from popular comedies of the period, including a clergyman, a governess, a preposterous potential mother-in-law (Lady Bracknell), false identities and improbable coincidences. But it differs from the entertainments of Arthur Wing Pinero and others by including a highly subversive sub-text about dishonesty in relationships, duplicity, masquerade and social-climbing, as well as the fatuousness and hypocrisies of high society, for those able to perceive it. Not all the critics did. William Archer, for one, having become accustomed to expect a serious message behind the comic sparkle of Oscar's plays failed to find it in this one. 'It is delightful to see, it sends wave after wave of laughter curling and foaming round the theatre; but as a text for criticism it is barren and delusive . . . What can a poor critic do with a play which raises no principle, whether of art or morals, creates its own canons and conventions, and is nothing but an absolutely wilful expression of an irrepressible witty personality?'[55]

Oscar was preoccupied with more pressing concerns than the critics' reactions. He had learned on his return from Algeria that the Marquess of Queensberry had booked a seat for the performance, so he instructed the theatre's business manager to return Queensberry's money with a note saying the performance was sold out. Queensberry's plan had been to stand up and address the audience, a disturbance that would have provoked a terrible scandal. Instead, as Oscar wrote to Bosie, *He left a grotesque bouquet of vegetables for me! This of course makes his conduct idiotic, robs it of dignity. He arrived with a prize fighter!! I had all Scotland Yard – twenty police – to guard the theatre. He prowled about for three hours, then left chattering like a monstrous ape.*[56] The insouciance of this note belies Oscar's true feelings, as the incident left him very shaken.

He was for the time being staying at the Avondale Hotel. He had lost all interest in family life and in his present state of mind could not even face Constance. His two little boys were away at prep school. Robbie Ross, ever the faithful friend, acted as a kind of go-between for messages between Constance and Oscar. When Bosie arrived back from Algeria, he moved into the Avondale with Oscar, but friction started almost immediately. When Bosie said he wanted a delightful rent boy he had found to move in with him as well, Oscar refused. His position was serious enough as it was, without attracting more unfavourable attention, but Bosie was incapable of understanding this, so he moved out in a huff.

Unbeknownst to either of them, Queensberry had meanwhile called at the Albemarle Club on 18 February, looking for Oscar. As Oscar was not there and the hall porter had no idea when he might drop by, Queensberry quickly scribbled a message on one of his visiting cards and handed it to the man to give to Oscar when next he came in. The handwriting was execrable and there is still some debate as to exactly what the note says, but the most common reading is 'For Oscar Wilde posing as somdomite [sic]'. It was 10 days before Oscar went to the Albemarle, where he was handed the card, which the porter had put into an envelope. His instant reaction was that things had now reached such a serious state that decisive action had to be taken. As he wrote to Robbie Ross, *Bosie's father has left a card at my club with hideous words in it. I don't see anything now but a criminal prosecution. My whole life seems ruined by this man. The tower of ivory is assailed by a foul thing.*[57] Queensberry had cleverly baited the trap, and Oscar had fallen right into it. More worried than penitent, Oscar sent a note off to Constance, saying that he would call round to see her at nine o'clock that evening. *Please be in – it is important.*[58]

First he went back to the Avondale Hotel, intending to check out and later travel to Paris, where he would be safe from further persecution from Queensberry. But he was unable to settle his bill and the manager refused to let him take away his luggage until he had. He therefore had no choice but to stay in London. He sent a note to Bosie, asking him to call round the following morning. First, though, he saw Robbie, who advised him to ignore the card, but Oscar maintained that he could not. Accordingly, the next morning he went to see the solicitor Robbie had earlier recommended, Charles Humphreys, taking Bosie with him. Bosie was exultant, seeing this as the opportunity he had been waiting for to hit back at his father for all his perceived faults and wrongdoing. The thought that a successful prosecution for libel might even lead to Queensberry being sent to jail was especially pleasing. Knowing Oscar could not afford to fund legal action himself, Bosie rashly assured him that his own mother and surviving elder brother Percy would pick up the bills. Humphreys was keen to take on the case, though he was not at all well versed in this type of litigation. Oscar and Bosie both assured him that there was no truth to Queensberry's allegations, in what would be the first of many lies. As events unfolded,

Edward Carson (1854–1935), later Baron Carson, had a distinguished career as both a lawyer and a politician. He practised on both sides of the Irish Sea, and was elected a Conservative and Unionist MP in Ireland. He stayed in the House of Commons for nearly 30 years. He was already Solicitor General of Ireland when he took on Queensberry's brief, and he went on to hold the same position in England, before becoming Attorney General, then First Lord of the Admiralty. As leader of the Irish Unionists, he was passionately opposed to the idea of Home Rule for Ireland.

Robbie Ross urged Oscar to be more open and honest with his legal counsels, but to no avail.

Accompanied by Bosie and Humphreys, Oscar went to Great Marlborough Street police station where a warrant was issued for Queensberry's arrest on the charge of publishing a libel against Oscar. The arrest was quickly effected and committal proceedings held, at which Sir George Lewis, for Queensberry, argued that his client would plead justification, in other words that his libellous remark was in the public interest because the allegation was true. Oscar and his solicitor should have been more alert to this warning signal, but Humphreys, believing Oscar and Bosie's lies, had no inkling of what might be coming. Queensberry had in fact for some time been using private detectives to collect evidence about Wilde's sexual activities, and was confident that he would be vindicated. His efforts to gather more incriminating material now redoubled.

Queensberry's committal proceedings opened on 9 March. Because of his friendship and past professional relationship with Oscar, George Lewis withdrew from the case as Queensberry's representative, being replaced by the ambitious Irish barrister, Edward Carson QC. By coincidence, Oscar had known Carson as a child, as well as at Trinity College, Dublin, as they were exact contemporaries. This in no way lessened the vigour with which Carson handled his client's defence, though it may briefly have lulled Oscar into a false sense of security. This may explain why Oscar succumbed at this highly inappropriate moment to Bosie's cajolery to take him to Monte Carlo for a few days' gambling at the casino. Quite apart from the fact that Oscar was not in a position to run up yet more debts, it was madness to go away on a foreign holiday with the Queensberry trial pending. It was even greater madness to come back.

The courtroom at the Old Bailey was packed when proceedings opened on 3 April. Dozens of lawyers in their wigs had crowded in to hear what they believed could prove to be an interesting case, as did many members of the Press. The public gallery contained some of Oscar's friends and supporters, but also rowdier elements who had come for some lively entertainment. The charge was that Queensberry had been 'contriving and maliciously intending to injure [Oscar Wilde] and to excite him to commit a breach of the peace and to bring him into public contempt scandal and disgrace.'

Sir Edward Clarke, the barrister briefed to prosecute on Oscar's behalf, having also been assured by his client that there was no substance to Queensberry's allegations, led Oscar gently through some aspects of his friendship with Bosie and the artistic nature of his writing. But when it was Carson's turn to cross-examine Oscar, he tripped him up immediately, by pointing out that whereas Oscar had declared that his age was 39, he was in fact 40. This silly example of petty vanity on Oscar's part inevitably put into question the reliability of the rest of his evidence. He was momentarily thrown, but later he regained his composure and started to venture witty quips, which played well to the gallery. When Carson read a short quotation from the original version of *The Picture of Dorian Gray* and asked him bluntly, 'Have you ever felt that feeling of adoring madly a beautiful male person many years younger than yourself?', Oscar replied, *I have never given any adoration to anybody except myself.*

On the second day of the libel trial, Carson delved more deeply into Oscar's private life. At first, the session went well. When Oscar said that iced champagne was his favourite drink, against his doctor's orders, Carson interjected, 'Never mind your doctor's orders!', to which Oscar retorted *I don't*. But the laughs from the spectators, who were more like a theatre audience than observers at a trial, subsided when Carson unsettled Oscar by asking about a young servant of Bosie's whom Oscar had known, Walter Grainger. 'Did you ever kiss him?' Carson asked sharply. *Oh no, never in my life. He was a peculiarly plain boy.* Like a terrier with a bone, Carson kept coming back to the issue of not kissing a boy because he was ugly. Oscar was no longer in command of the courtroom. And as it became clear that Queensberry had rounded up a startling group of rent boys and others who could testify to Oscar's sexual adventures, Sir Edward Clarke felt he had to recommend to Oscar that he withdraw the prosecution. So much had already come out, however, that it was inevitable that the papers from the trial would be studied to see if a prosecution should now be launched against Oscar himself.

Naturally, he felt despondent and disoriented. Though Oscar's lawyers had assured the authorities that their client would not leave the country while the Director of Public Prosecution decided whether to open a case against him, most of Oscar's friends clamoured for him to escape before it was too late. Constance and Robbie Ross were among those urging him to leave, while on the opposite side, Bosie and Speranza were insisting that he should stay. Lady Wilde considered this to be a matter of honour, and was quite sure he would be victorious if there were to be a case. When George Alexander had earlier recommended that Oscar flee abroad, Oscar had replied flippantly, *Everybody wants me to go abroad. I have just been abroad. One can't keep on going abroad, unless one is a missionary or, what comes to the same thing, a commercial traveller.*[59] Now his capacity for humour was reduced, and he spent a good part of his last day of freedom slumped in a chair in a room at the Cadogan Hotel in Sloane Street, drinking. That was how he was

Oscar Wilde in the year of his trial

found when detectives called to take him away. He was charged at Bow Street Magistrates Court under the Criminal Law Amendment Act of 1885, alongside Alfred Taylor, the young gentleman who had procured boys for him. Nobly, Taylor refused an offer from the prosecution to turn Queen's evidence against him.

Oscar was refused bail and was held as a remand prisoner at Holloway for a month. Conditions for remand prisoners were reasonably comfortable. He occupied what was called a special cell, which was bigger than the norm, about 11 feet square; occupants could have furniture and meals of their own choosing sent in and they were allowed to dress in their own clothes. Nonetheless Oscar's spirits were often low, not least when he heard that Queensberry had forced a bankruptcy sale of the contents of his Tite Street house, many of which went for a song in an unseemly scramble. Fortunately Robbie Ross, as soon as Oscar had been arrested, had rushed to the house and got Oscar's servant to break into the study, so he had been able to remove many compromising papers and manuscripts. But hundreds of signed presentation copies of books that Oscar had received, as well as pictures and other beautiful objects, were scattered, never to be recovered. Constance had removed herself from the house well before this. She sent Cyril and Vyvyan to Switzerland, and soon followed to the continent herself. The one thing that kept Oscar from total despair, or so he told friends like Ada Leverson, were the regular visits he received from Bosie Douglas. *A slim thing, gold-haired like an angel, stands always at my side. His presence overshadows me. He moves in the gloom like a white flower.*[60]

Oscar's first trial as defendant, which opened on 26 April, was an excruciating affair. He and Alfred Taylor were charged on 25 counts of gross indecency, involving several of the rent boys whom Oscar had indeed been to bed with, as well as the publisher's clerk Edward Shelley. Bosie's name was not cited and it is highly likely that Queensberry had used his influence to try to keep his son out of the proceedings. As they progressed, nonetheless, Oscar's legal team judged that it would be prudent for Bosie to leave the country; he headed for France, as did Robbie Ross. According to Frank Harris, hundreds of men who had secret homosexual lives that might be exposed in any post-trial witch-hunt also took the opportunity of boarding available ferries. Much sordid evidence was produced in court, from chambermaids and others, involving soiled sheets and other signs of 'unnatural' practices. Several of the boys gave testimony, some more credibly than others. With a few exceptions, they formed a sad parade of rent boys and blackmailers, some of whom, it later transpired, were getting financial assistance from Queensberry to be present for the duration of the trial.

Oscar himself was not called into the witness box until 30 April, when Sir Edward Clarke – who had agreed to defend Oscar without a fee – did his best to help Oscar portray his effusive written appreciation of young men as a spiritual or aesthetic rather than carnal matter. In his cross-examination, Arthur Gill for the Crown quoted from Bosie's reference to the 'love that dare not speak its name', in his sonnet 'Two Loves', and asked whether this was not a clear reference to unnatural love. This touched on a subject dear to Oscar's heart, enabling him to deliver extempore an eloquent defence of same sex love between an older and a younger man. This, Oscar argued, was neither ugly nor unnatural. Moreover, writings of his own, such as *The Picture of Dorian Gray*, as well as

The Love that dare not speak its name is such a great affection of an elder man for a younger man as there was between David and Jonathan, such as Plato made the very basis of his philosophy, and such as you would find in the sonnets of Michelangelo and Shakespeare . . . It is in this century misunderstood, so much misunderstood that it may be described as the 'Love that dare not speak its name', and on account of it I am placed where I am now. It is beautiful, it is fine, it is the noblest form of affection. There is nothing unnatural about it.

his letters to Bosie, a couple of which had been read out in court, should, he said, be seen in that light. Oscar's speech – for it was a speech – was greeted with spontaneous applause from the public gallery, causing the judge to threaten to clear the court. The power of the speech may also have been one reason why the jury, after nearly four hours of deliberation on 1 May, failed to reach a verdict. For the moment, the case had collapsed.

Bail was granted, at the colossal sum of £5,000, which was put up by Bosie's brother Percy and an altruistic Anglican clergyman by the name of Stewart Headlam. After the bail hearing, on 7 May, Oscar was released and headed for the Midland Hotel at St Pancras, only to be evicted by the management after a few hours. Nowhere else would take him in, as some of Queensberry's thugs were pursuing him, so he ended up seeking sanctuary in his mother's small house in Oakley Street, Chelsea, where his brother Willie and his second wife were also living. Oscar found it quite unbearable being in such close quarters with Willie under the circumstances, as he found his brother to be crass and insensitive, even when he was trying to be kind. With great relief, therefore, Oscar accepted an invitation to go to stay with Ada Leverson and her husband Ernest instead. Ernest Leverson had already proved to be a valuable support, even though he did not know Oscar particularly well, as he had advanced Oscar £500 to help with his legal costs.

Messages of support came in from several Irish writers, though interestingly not from many English ones. Again several friends urged him to flee; Frank Harris reportedly had a yacht waiting for him down the Thames, ready to spirit him out of the country. But he stayed. He may have hoped that the case would eventually be dropped, but powerful voices in the Liberal Party were arguing that the prosecution must go ahead and ideally should succeed. Otherwise, it was feared, the Marquess of Queensberry would make sure that the spotlight fell on the Prime Minister, Lord Rosebery, instead.

The second trial opened at the Old Bailey on 20 May and was largely a rerun of the first, but with the Solicitor General Sir Frank Lockwood leading the prosecution. The Judge this time was Sir Alfred Wills, a reactionary figure who was hardly likely to be sympathetic to Oscar. The same cast of boys from the underworld played their parts, but there was little fresh eloquence from Oscar. On 25 May, the foreman of the jury interrupted the judge's summing up to ask whether any warrant had been issued for Lord Alfred Douglas's arrest. The answer was negative, but it was an ominous sign. A guilty verdict now seemed inevitable. This is indeed what happened, on all counts except the one relating to Edward Shelley. Turning to Oscar and Alfred Taylor – who had been tried separately earlier, but was sentenced at the same time – Mr Justice Wills declared: 'It is no use for me to address you. People who can do these things must be dead to all sense of shame, and one cannot hope to produce any effect upon them. It is the worst case I have ever tried. That you, Taylor, kept a kind of male brothel it is impossible to doubt. And that you, Wilde, have been the centre of a circle of extensive corruption of the most hideous kind among young men, it is equally impossible to doubt. I shall, under the circumstances, be expected to pass the severest sentence that the law allows. In my judgement it is totally inadequate for such a case as this. The sentence of the Court is that each of you be imprisoned and kept to hard labour for two years.'[61]

A lone voice cried out 'Shame!' but there was applause from other sections of the public gallery, as Oscar, looking dazed, was quickly bundled down to the cells. Legend has it that outside in the street, female prostitutes danced with joy, as Oscar had allegedly made sex with boys fashionable in some quarters, harming their trade. The Marquess of Queensberry that evening took some of his cronies off for a celebratory dinner.

Much of the Press was merciless. The *News of the World* crowed, 'The aesthetic cult, in the nasty form, is over', while the *Daily Telegraph* trumpeted, 'Open the windows! Let in the fresh air.'[62] It was left to the popular newspaper *Reynolds's News* to

The trial of Oscar Wilde created endless lurid headlines

point out that Oscar had corrupted none of the young men who appeared in the witness box, and its editorial refused to join in the Fleet Street gloating over 'the ruin of an unhappy man.'[63]

From the Old Bailey's cells Oscar was conveyed back to Holloway where he was made to take a bath and was issued with a set of prison clothes, stamped with the traditional broad arrows. On 9 June, he was transferred to Pentonville, where he was given a thorough medical examination, before being declared fit to undergo his physical punishment of six hours daily on a treadmill – 20 minutes on, then five minutes off – for a whole month. It was an exhausting torment for a bulky man who had rarely taken physical exercise since leaving university, but even more unbearable was the low-level plank bed on which he had to sleep – or rather, doze fitfully, as chronic insomnia set in. The food was execrable, and guaranteed to provoke diarrhoea. As the prisoners were locked in their cells all night, with only a tin container as a primitive sanitary arrangement, the stench the guards encountered when they unlocked the cells in the morning would sometimes make them retch.

After the first month, Oscar was set to picking oakum, a loose fibre used mainly in caulking and obtained by pulling old rope to pieces. This was a mindless mechanical task, which he executed very badly. For an hour a day, he was able to exercise outside, walking slowly in line with other prisoners, who were forbidden to talk to each other. For the first three months, Oscar was not allowed to communicate with anyone outside the prison. He had no reading material, other than the Bible and John Bunyan's *The Pilgrim's Progress*, nor a pen nor paper. Under this strict regime, he rapidly lost weight, which was in itself no bad thing; but psychologically, the effect of his incarceration and the lack of mental stimulation or human warmth were devastating. One of his fellow prisoners, who had learnt the art of speaking without the guards being able to see his lips move, muttered one day in the exercise yard, 'I am sorry for you: it is harder for the likes of you than it is for the likes of us.'[64]

Oscar's first outside visitor was a member of the Home Office committee investigating prisons, Richard Burdon Haldane (1856–1928), a Scottish jurist and Liberal MP who went on to become Lord Chancellor. He had known Oscar before his downfall, but was encouraged to look at how Oscar was faring by a friend of Constance

Wilde's, Margaret Brooke, the Ranee of Sarawak. Haldane could not resist giving Oscar a little moral lecture, by suggesting that he had not yet used his great literary gift to its full force because he had dissipated himself in a life of pleasure. 'Now misfortune might prove a blessing for his career, for he had got a great subject,' Haldane later recalled. The idea seemed to appeal to Oscar, but it was Haldane's promise to try to arrange for him to have other books to read that prompted Oscar to cry with gratitude. Together they drew up an eclectic little list of five titles by St Augustine, Blaise Pascal, Walter Pater, Theodore Mommsen and Cardinal Newman. The books did not arrive until mid-August, by which time Oscar had been transferred to Wandsworth Prison, where they were added to the library to be at his disposal.

Robert Sherard, who had moved to England in the hope of furthering his writing career, happened to live near Wandsworth Prison, and was the first of Oscar's friends to be allowed to visit him, towards the end of August. Sherard found Oscar to be a changed man from the flamboyant figure he had known in Paris. His hair was unkempt and he had grown a straggly beard. His face was thin and his hands were disfigured, his nails broken and bleeding from picking oakum. Sherard had unwelcome news of Bosie Douglas, who was still living in France and was intending to publish an article in the French literary review *Mercure de France*, incorporating quotes from three of Oscar's love letters. Oscar urged Sherard to stop him at all costs.

Constance had been threatening to divorce him, but had recanted out of pity, and even suggested that after his release, he might be reunited with her and the two boys. She confirmed this when she travelled from Switzerland to see Oscar on 25 September, despite the fact that she was in quite serious pain from an old back injury incurred when she fell down the stairs at Tite Street. Like Sherard, she was dismayed by Oscar's appearance and she was distressed that the visiting room was laid out in such a way that she could not touch him. Any new revelations about the nature of his relationship with Bosie could jeopardise the possibility of the family being reunited. After several agonising months in prison, Oscar no longer felt love for Bosie. With every day that passed, his resentment grew over the way Bosie's behaviour had directly led to his current predicament. He told Constance that if he saw Lord Alfred now, he would kill him.[65]

Oscar was let out of jail just twice, on 24 September and 12 November, when he had to attend bankruptcy proceedings. He had outstanding debts of over £3,500 pounds, of which £677 were legal costs awarded to the Marquess of Queensberry. It was Queensberry who now pressed for Oscar to be declared bankrupt; as a rich man, he did not need the money, but his spite was boundless. Robbie Ross tried to raise enough money from Oscar's friends to clear off the debts and avert the bankruptcy, but as soon as people got wind of the scheme, new creditors kept emerging, and Robbie had to admit defeat. He travelled over especially to England in November to stand in the corridor outside the bankruptcy court. As Oscar was led past, he solemnly raised his hat in silent tribute.

Oscar had spent most of the period between the two visits to the bankruptcy court in the infirmary at Wandsworth Prison, being treated for dysentery. He also had an infected ear, which he had injured when he fainted in the prison chapel. When R B Haldane visited him again, Oscar caused him sufficient concern for Haldane to recommend that he be moved out of Wandsworth, where some of the warders had a reputation for brutality and for treating the less compliant prisoners as malingerers. Accordingly, on 21 November, Oscar was transferred to Reading Gaol.

The actual transfer was the most traumatic experience of Oscar's sentence. He and his accompanying guards had to travel by train, which involved changing trains at Clapham Junction. They had quite a long wait on the platform for the connection,

The regime at Reading Gaol was easier for Wilde to endure than that at Pentonville and Wandsworth

and as commuters passing through recognised the large man standing there, handcuffed and in prison garb, they started to laugh and jeer. One man walked up to him and spat in his face. Oscar had recurring nightmares about the incident.

At first, Reading did not seem to be any real improvement over Wandsworth. The Governor at the time was a martinet by the name of Lieutenant Colonel Henry Isaacson (1842–1915), who believed in the curative nature of punishment. Even small infringements of prison regulations, such as failing to comply with the precise pattern in which the few objects in a prisoner's cell should be placed, could incur the Governor's wrath, and lead to the withdrawal of the most basic privileges. Oscar summed up Colonel Isaacson as having *the eyes of a ferret, the body of an ape, and the soul of a rat*. However, the physical regime at Reading was easier than that at Wandsworth: Oscar was detailed to work in the garden, and to act as a library orderly, taking books to other prisoners. He was able to spend time in his cell reading, but he had still not been given permission to write, except for a very small quota of letters, after which pen and paper were taken away. The library was not well endowed with the sort of books that would interest him, but he was able to order some more, including a Greek lexicon, a Latin dictionary and an Italian primer. He had decided to teach himself Italian in preparation for his eventual release from prison, as he knew there was no realistic chance of his being able to continue living in Britain.

Yet his reputation was not completely tarnished. Though his name had been taken off the billboards outside the two London theatres where his two last plays were being performed at the time of his trial, and the plays themselves were taken off shortly afterwards, some of his work was starting to reappear. In May 1895, shortly after the trials, the bookseller Arthur Humphreys at Hatchard's in Piccadilly – the man who may have had a little fling with Constance before Oscar's disgrace – brought out a new edition of Oscar's long essay on Socialism, now titled simply *The Soul of Man*. In October, a new edition of *Dorian Gray* appeared. And most encouragingly, in February 1896, Aurélien-Marie Lugné-Poë (1869–1940) produced *Salomé* at the Théâtre de l'Oeuvre in Paris. The play was received rapturously, as Aubrey Beardsley, who was in the audience, was able to report. News of this filtered into the prison. Though it does not seem to have softened Colonel Isaacson's heart, it did raise Oscar's status among some of his fellow prisoners and the warders.

A week after *Salomé* opened in Paris, Oscar had another visit from Constance, who was by this time living in Genoa. She had travelled especially from Italy to inform him that his mother had died, but he told her that he had had a premonitory dream about this, so the news came as no surprise. During her last illness, Lady Wilde has asked if Oscar could be allowed out to see her, but the prison authorities refused, so mother and son never had the chance to say farewell.

Petitions requesting that Oscar should be released early from prison, on compassionate grounds, equally fell on deaf ears. As the days dragged slowly by, Oscar's greatest fear was that he would go mad.

Prison chaplains – who could visit prisoners whenever they wanted – were no consolation. The one at Pentonville had been particularly prissy. 'Mr Wilde, did you have morning prayers in your house?' he once asked. *I am sorry. I fear not.* 'You see where you are now!' the chaplain retorted triumphantly. Similarly, when the chaplain at Reading visited Oscar in his cell and Oscar complained that he could not see the sky through the cloudy glass of his cell window, the chaplain responded, 'Oh my friend, let me entreat you to desist from such thoughts and not let your mind dwell on the clouds, but on Him who is above the clouds, Him who . . .' He got no further, as Oscar angrily pushed him out of the cell shouting *Get out, you damned fool!* That act of insubordination earned him another punishment.

Daily attendance at chapel – twice on Sundays – was compulsory for all prisoners, except for those who were seriously ill. But Oscar got no comfort from the services. He did, however, increasingly turn his mind to religion, and in particular to the example of Jesus Christ. One cannot know whether Oscar ever prayed that Colonel Isaacson would be removed from his life, but if he did, his prayer was answered. In July 1896, Isaacson was replaced by a Major James Nelson (1859–1914). Five years younger than Oscar, Major Nelson was a far more enlightened man than his predecessor and belonged to a new generation of prison governors, who rejected the prevailing view of the beneficial effect of 'hard labour, hard board and hard fare' in favour of a more modern approach, which treated prisoners as human beings who needed to develop their good nature. Oscar later referred to him as a Christ-like man, and burst into tears of relief the first time he met him.

Nelson bent the prison rules creatively, so that Oscar's right to write an occasional letter was interpreted as permission to compose

The prison-system is absolutely and entirely wrong. I would give anything to be able to alter it when I go out. I intend to try. But there is nothing in the world so wrong but that the spirit of Humanity, which is the spirit of Love, the spirit of the Christ who is not in Churches, may make it, if not right, at least possible to be borne without too much bitterness of heart. I know also that much is waiting for me outside that is very delightful, from what St Francis of Assisi calls 'my brother the wind' and 'my sister the rain', lovely things both of them, down to the shop-windows and sunsets of great cities.

one of his longest pieces of prose: a memoir in the form of an epistle to Lord Alfred Douglas, to which Robbie Ross would later give the title *De Profundis*. For three months, Oscar worked on the text, pouring out all his grievances against Bosie and recriminations for their extravagant lifestyle, but also developing some of his religious ideas. Convinced of Oscar's literary talent, Major Nelson hoped the project could turn into another *Pilgrim's Progress*. Prison rules stipulated that letters still in composition could not be kept in cells overnight, so each evening, the paper that Oscar had been working on was taken away and in principle could not be returned. But it seems as if the rules were bent again, as several sections of the manuscript of *De Profundis* show extensive revision.

Written between January and March 1897, *De Profundis* is to an extent an act of confession, for even if Oscar places much of the blame for the excesses that led to his imprisonment on Bosie's shoulders, he recognises some of his own character weaknesses. Writing it proved to be a highly therapeutic exercise, both in helping him take control of himself, and in purging himself of his ill feelings towards Bosie. The latter had been exacerbated by reports Oscar had of Bosie's behaviour abroad, and his realisation that Bosie was entirely selfish. For a while, indeed, Oscar came to believe that Bosie was evil.

As the date of Oscar's release started to loom, he became increasingly concerned about how he would survive. Under his marriage settlement with Constance, he had a life interest on half of her dowry. But because of his bankruptcy, this had passed into the hands of the Official Receiver, who put it up for sale. Constance tried to buy it back, but Robbie Ross and another of Oscar's friends, More Adey, outbid her solicitor's offer. This caused considerable resentment all round. In addition, Constance had agreed to pay Oscar £200 a year as an allowance on his release, but there was now talking of reducing this to £150. In his anxiety and solitude, Oscar began to suspect various friends, including Ernest Leverson, of not acting in his best interest, and of interfering in his affairs.

Oscar's final months in prison were considerably alleviated by a friendship he developed with a kind warder, Thomas Martin, who slipped him a copy of the *Daily Chronicle* each morning. Martin's kind-heartedness would eventually cost him his job, as he was fired for slipping a biscuit to a child prisoner whom he found crying. Oscar was charmed by Martin's simplicity, while Martin and some of the other warders looked up to Oscar, and started consulting him on literary matters. One asked him one day whether the popular novelist Marie Corelli (1855–1924) would be considered a great writer. Oscar leant over and put his hand on the warder's shoulder and said, *Now don't think I've anything against her moral character, but from the way she writes* she ought to be here.[66]

Oscar's spirits soared as the day of his release approached. This was scheduled for 19 May, but bureaucratic procedures determined that it should happen from the prison in which he was first incarcerated, which was considered to be Pentonville. He therefore had to be moved from Reading to London the previous day. The plan was to do this as discreetly as possible, to try to limit Press interest, though two journalists did show up to cover his departure from Reading. He was allowed to travel in his own clothes, and was not handcuffed, partly in the forlorn hope that nobody would recognise him on the journey. Major Nelson handed him the complete manuscript of *De Profundis* as he left. He was driven off in a cab with two prison officers to Twyford station. While standing on the platform, waiting for the train, Oscar spotted a flowering bush in bud and stretched his arms out to it exclaiming, *Oh beautiful world! Oh beautiful world!* 'Now, Mr Wilde,' one of the officers rebuked him, 'you mustn't give yourself away like that. You're the only man in England who would talk like that on a railway station!'[67]

Exile

To get back my youth I would do anything in the world,
except take exercise, get up early or be respectable.

There is a widespread myth that Oscar Wilde emerged from prison a broken man, a martyr to Victorian prejudice and hypocrisy. But the truth is much more complex. The privations of jail and the sadistic nature of its regime undoubtedly shortened Oscar's life, but they also added a new dimension to it. He claimed himself to have learned two lessons from the experience: humility and pity. Oscar before the fall had been a fundamentally kind man, but vain, fired with a burning ambition to make his mark, to conquer the world, or at least the parts of the world that mattered to him – England, America and France. He had known great success and temporary wealth, but he had not known how to handle them. He had experienced love, but had found it to be an often painful condition. Now he had regained his freedom, he had to discover what really mattered in life, to savour it during the time he had left.

On his discharge from Pentonville, early on the morning of 19 May 1897, he was taken to Stewart Headlam's house, a reassuring environment with its 1880s decor, William Morris wallpaper and curtains, and pictures by Rossetti and Burne-Jones. Oscar reflected that most of the important people in his past life, including the three to whom he once claimed to be 'married' – Constance, Robbie and Bosie – were abroad, or – in the case of his beloved mother – dead. He had long ago turned his back on his homeland, Ireland, but many of his links with England had also now been severed. His house had gone, along with almost all of his possessions, and the doors of London Society would remain closed. There was nothing to detain him. He had anyway lived largely in hotel rooms and out of suitcases during the two years prior to being sent to prison. Now he would do so again, but abroad.

It is not surprising that Oscar was in a philosophical mood on that May morning, as he prepared to face the world. For a moment, the prospect was too daunting and he had a note sent round to a Jesuit community in Farm Street, asking to go on a six-month religious retreat. He was in effect asking to prolong his incarceration, albeit in more human surroundings, in an institution with strict rules and discipline. But the Jesuits turned him down, worried that his approach was too hasty, and based on fear rather than faith. He had to learn how to stand on his own feet again, as well as finding some new reason to live.

There were still some friends whom he valued, people who had not destroyed his letters or torn up his photographs, as many had done, in an effort to expunge Oscar and his 'sins' from their lives. As he made clear in *De Profundis*, he had learned to become more discriminating about people, to realise who really were men and women of value, rather than boon companions or fair-weather friends. Among his first visitors at Stewart Headlam's that morning was Ada Leverson, the woman the pre-trial Oscar had called 'the Sphinx'. She had gone to great trouble to make herself look as elegant as possible for this reunion and she was delighted to find that the man she and her companions had come to see seemed largely to be his old self. 'We all felt intensely nervous and embarrassed,' she later recalled. 'We had the English fear of showing our feelings, and at the same time the human fear of not showing our feelings.' Oscar strode into the room with the dignity of a king returning from exile, talking, laughing and brandishing a cigarette. He had a flower in his buttonhole, 'and he looked markedly better, slighter and younger than he had two years previously.'[68]

So many people came to see Oscar that morning and he was in such voluble form that he missed the train that connected with the afternoon ferry. This meant that he had to travel for most of the night, arriving in Dieppe at four o'clock in the morning. Robbie Ross and Reggie Turner were on the quayside to meet him; solemnly Oscar handed over to Robbie an envelope containing the manuscript of *De Profundis*, which he was to have copied, so one copy could be sent to Bosie and the other retained. Robbie and Reggie had had a room prepared for him at the Hôtel Sandwich in Dieppe, filled with flowers, books and other presents and the heartening news that Robbie had managed to raise about £800 from friends and well-wishers to tide him over while he resuscitated his writing career. No one ever imagined he would or could do anything else. He was not the sort of person to finance his life abroad by giving English lessons.

Officially, as far as hotel proprietors, tradesmen and strangers were concerned, Oscar had a new identity, as Mr Sebastian Melmoth. The alias had been chosen with care. *Melmoth the Wanderer* was the title of the most famous novel by Oscar's great-uncle, Charles Robert Maturin, a convoluted but at times powerful book that involved, like *The Picture of Dorian Gray*, a compact with the Devil. Sebastian was Oscar's favourite saint, the martyr whose body, pierced with arrows, had become a homoerotic icon in the works of several painters. Reggie Turner had had travelling bags made for Oscar, stamped with the initials SM.

Not that this simple disguise fooled the many English visitors to the then fashionable resort of Dieppe. When Oscar went into restaurants, or even walked the streets of the town, he found himself being repeatedly snubbed. Diners asked maître d's to have him removed, or else left in noisy protest. Even some of Oscar's former friends did not wish to be seen with him in public. One day Oscar spotted Aubrey Beardsley, in the company of the two painters Charles Condor and Jacques-Emile Blanche, hurrying away. One person was keen to see him: Bosie Douglas. A letter soon arrived at Oscar's hotel from Bosie. He said he had heard that Oscar now hated him, but he continued to love his friend. Oscar replied that he did still love Bosie – the pendulum of his emotions having swung again – but that it was better for them not to meet. The letters from Bosie continued to arrive, now cajoling, now insulting, now pledging eternal devotion and a wish to atone for the disaster that had brought Oscar down.

Oscar was keen to avoid getting back into the position he was in before his imprisonment, when Bosie had put him under such immense strain, financial and psychological. Moreover, he had some projects he wanted to work on. In light-hearted conversation with Robbie he had turned Reading Gaol into a kind of fairyland, in which Major Nelson was a benign gentleman who presided over an enchanted garden. But there was a much crueller side to real prison life, even under Major Nelson, which Oscar wanted to expose. In Dieppe, he wrote a very long letter condemning the practice of imprisoning young children, often for quite trivial offences like catching a rabbit or stealing a loaf of bread. He sent it to the *Daily Chronicle*, which published it on 28 May. *A child can understand a punishment inflicted by an individual, such as a parent or guardian,* he argued, *and bear it with a certain amount of acquiescence. What it cannot understand is a punishment inflicted by society. It cannot realise what society is. With grown people, it is of course, the reverse.*[69]

The letter caused considerable comment and undoubtedly contributed to the cause of prison reform. But Oscar also had in mind a much more substantial work, which would not just be a polemic, but rather a work of art. Again, the inspiration was something he had witnessed at first hand at Reading. On 7 July

1896, one of the prisoners, a soldier by the name of Charles Wooldridge, was hanged in the grounds of the prison for the premeditated murder of his wife. The execution deeply troubled Oscar, and became the focal point of a lengthy poem he wanted to write, in which Wooldridge's experience of prison and his own would be intertwined: *The Ballad of Reading Gaol*. Oscar needed a tranquil place to compose this work and was delighted to discover the small seaside community of Berneval, just a few miles along the coast from Dieppe. In summer, the place looked inviting and there was a beach from which he could swim. On 26 May he moved into the village and Robbie Ross helped him settle in, before proceeding to London. Oscar soon became a kind of fairy godfather to the local children, organising a highly successful party for 15 little boys to mark Queen Victoria's birthday on 23 June, at which strawberries and cream were served, with cakes, and every child chose a musical instrument as a present.

Most of the *Ballad* was written during July, though Oscar would later expand it so it could be published in book form, pseudonymously, under the name C 3 3, the number of his own cell, and therefore his official identity, at Reading. Oscar had plenty of visitors in Berneval that summer, including Robert Sherard, André Gide and the poet Ernest Dowson, and he contemplated having a villa built so he could have the village as a permanent base.

At the same time, he settled into a pattern of affectionate correspondence with Bosie, who was once more 'My dear Boy' in letters. Oscar recounted with

I walked, with other souls in pain,
  Within another ring,
And was wondering if the man had done
  A great or little thing,
When a voice behind me whispered low,
  'That fellow's got to swing.'

With midnight always in one's heart,
  And twilight in one's cell,
We turn the crank, or tear the rope,
  Each in his separate Hell,
And the silence is more awful far
  Than the sound of the brazen bell.

gusto his life at Berneval, while keeping Bosie at bay. Nonetheless, towards the end of August, Oscar did agree to meet up with Bosie in Rouen. This turned out to be a passionate reunion; a couple of days later, Oscar was writing to him that *my only hope of again doing beautiful work in art is being with you. It was not so in old days, but now it is different, and you can really recreate in me that energy and sense of joyous power on which art depends.*[70]

Oscar was aware that he could not keep this reconciliation secret, though he tried to fool Robbie for some time about his true feelings for Bosie. When Robbie found out what was going on, he was angry and hurt, feeling Oscar was undermining all the work he had been doing to give him a solid base for rebuilding his life. Constance was furious. She had really begun to hope that Oscar was a reformed man and that it would be possible after all for him to live with her and to become father to the boys once again. She railed at him in a letter, categorically forbidding him to see Bosie again, but it was no use. Although Oscar knew that he was jeopardising the income he received from her and risking that he would never again see his two children, the pull of Bosie was too strong. As Oscar wrote to Robbie, *My going back to Bosie was psychologically inevitable: and, setting aside the interior life of the soul with its passion for self-realisation at all costs, the world forced it on me. I cannot live without the atmosphere of Love: I must love and be loved, whatever price I pay for it.*[71]

Oscar packed up his belongings in Berneval, settled his bills with some of the fast-diminishing pot of money that Robbie had collected for him and joined Bosie in Naples. They rented a villa at Posillipo, just outside the city, and made trips to Capri and surrounding beauty spots. Oscar finished off *The Ballad of Reading Gaol*, which he had arranged to have published by one of the seminal figures of fin-de-siècle literary London, Leonard Smithers (1861–1907). Oscar had also persuaded the affluent composer and pianist Dalhousie Young (1866–1921) to give him a £100 advance for a libretto for a proposed Young opera on the theme of Daphnis and Chloe. Working together, Oscar and Bosie did manage to come up with a few dismal lyrics, but the libretto was never completed. However, Oscar was so pleased with the way that making such a suggestion produced money that he tried similar tactics over the next couple of years with other likely sponsors of several other putative projects, which also did not come to fruition.

The main source of income for both Oscar and Bosie, however, was the allowances they got from Constance and Lady Queensberry respectively. In Bosie's case this amounted to a very generous £25 a week, though, given his extravagant nature, even this was not enough. Neither he nor Oscar had either the will or the ability to stay within their budgets. At the villa in Posillipo, for example, they employed four servants, and they frequently went out to the theatre or to restaurants, continuing their tradition of eating and drinking only the best. Independently but simultaneously, Constance and Lady Queensberry decided to use their financial clout to separate the reunited lovers, by informing them that their allowances would be stopped unless they ceased living together. Lady Queensberry went so far as to offer to clear Bosie's Neapolitan debts and to give Oscar an outright sum of £200 if they signed an agreement to this effect. It was an offer the two men could not afford to refuse. But their acceptance also implies that the love that bound them was not as strong as it had been in the past, notably from Bosie's side. In early December, Bosie left for Rome, while Oscar stayed on in Naples. They would never live together again, though their paths crossed frequently. Constance, meanwhile, had abandoned all hope of a reconciliation with Oscar, writing to Arthur Humphreys that 'his punishment has not done him much good since it has not taught him the lesson he most needed, namely that he is not the only person in the world.'[72] There was now no chance Oscar would ever see his sons again. Even their surname had been legally changed, to Holland –

one of Constance's family names – largely to shield the boys from public curiosity, but also to underline Oscar's loss of paternal rights.

Oscar lingered in Naples until the beginning of February, by which time he was almost completely penniless. He decided he had no alternative but to move to Paris, where he could live more cheaply and he had more friends. By the middle of the month, he was settled in the Hôtel de Nice on the rue des Beaux-Arts, on the Left Bank. There was then a timely improvement in his fortunes, as *The Ballad of Reading Gaol* had been published and sold briskly. Over the next three months, it ran to seven impressions, as well as a limited edition of 99 copies, signed by Oscar with his real name. The *Ballad* was widely reviewed, with none of the critics revealing the identity of the book's author, though it was hardly a well-guarded secret. Most gave qualified praise. The *Pall Mall Gazette* called it the most remarkable poem to have appeared that year, while Arthur Symons, writing in the *Saturday Review*, highlighted with approval the poem's refrain that all men kill the thing they love. 'This symbol of the obscure deaths of the heart, the unseen violence upon souls, the martyrdom of hope, trust and all the more helpless among the virtues, is what gives it its unity.'[73]

The success of the *Ballad* gave Oscar the ideal opportunity to relaunch his literary career, but as he confessed to friends, he had lost the joy of writing. He came up with various ideas to write some religious plays, which came to nought, and he drafted a scenario for a social comedy, which he sold to Frank Harris, who turned it into *Mr and Mrs Daventry*. Unfortunately, he sold the same scenario to other people as well, which caused some friction. One task he did manage to finish, however, was the editing for publication of his last two plays, *An Ideal Husband* and *The Importance of Being Earnest*, which were brought out by Leonard Smithers.

In Paris, Oscar established a lifestyle that was a pale mirror of his pre-trial London existence. He rose late, sometimes in mid-afternoon, and would usually settle at one of the outside tables of a boulevard café for a few hours, where he could sit over a single drink of yellow advocaat or the more pernicious green absinthe. When he was in funds, often immediately after a visit by Robbie Ross, who acted as a kind of banker, he would have champagne. The great advantage of the boulevard cafés was that one could watch the world go by and hail passing friends, especially if they were the sort who would be likely to buy one a drink. One evening in the late summer or early autumn of 1898, he called out to André Gide, when he saw the young man walking past. André was shocked by what he saw as Oscar's deterioration. It was not just that his clothes were no longer as smart and soigné as they had been in the past, or that his health did not look all that good. It was as if his personality had shrunk. He was no longer a man with a bright future, but a man with a tainted past. Gide sat down with Oscar, but with his back turned to the street. Oscar immediately realised this was to avoid being seen in public with him, and remonstrated. But soon Oscar's humour improved, and he started regaling Gide with stories, as in the old days.

Though by no means universally acceptable in Paris Society, Oscar had a far better social life in the French capital than he could ever have enjoyed in London following his disgrace. Moreover, many young French writers sought out his company – sometimes leaving him to pay the bill when he had cash – giving him the respect due to an acknowledged master. As ever, Oscar was stimulated by the company of young men. He often claimed that he could only learn from the young. But he was not looking for another talented gilded youth with whom to share his life. Instead, he formed an affectionate relationship with a young and charming soldier called Maurice Gilbert, who was a frequent companion. Gilbert also got passed around several of Oscar's homosexual friends in London. The practice of sharing reliable youths had become quite common in England, as one way of trying to avoid blackmail.

The moral climate in Paris was far more liberal, and now that Oscar had no reputation to lose, he took full advantage of it. One French acquaintance was shocked one day to come across Oscar kissing Maurice Gilbert in public. Oscar also revived his habit of having relations with rent boys, of whom there were plenty cruising the boulevards. Oscar was quite philosophical about it, telling Robbie Ross, *How evil it is to buy Love, and how evil to sell it! And yet what purple hours one can snatch from that grey slow-moving thing we call Time! My mouth is twisted with kissing, and I feed on fevers.*[74] One reason Robbie doled out money to Oscar in regular, small amounts was that he knew Oscar well enough to realise that if he gave him a significant sum, Oscar would most likely splurge most of it on some boy.

Having been phenomenally generous, indeed spendthrift, when he had money before his downfall, Oscar had no qualms about enjoying the hospitality of friends, or even strangers, and on occasions would openly solicit them for cash. He became quite a proficient wheedler when it came to getting money out of people, though sometimes he would forget that he had already used one pretext with a person and embarrass them and himself by trying the same tack a second time. A born actor, who used the world as his stage, he honed to perfection the role of indigent. He accosted the Australian opera singer Nellie Melba (1861–1931) in a Paris street once. She was so moved by his hard luck story that she opened her handbag and turned it upside down over his open hands. When confronted with such a windfall, Oscar would, as often or not, take himself off to a restaurant for a slap-up meal.

He also benefited from the hospitality of several rich friends and acquaintances, even if their idea of entertaining did not always meet his exacting standards. Frank Harris, who had substantial interests on the Riviera, invited Oscar down to Napoule over Christmas 1898, though when Oscar got there, Oscar discovered that Harris was not coming after all, so he was left to his own devices in the hotel room Harris had provided. Oscar had no reason to complain, as he had discovered, so he informed Robbie, that *the fishing population of the Riviera have the same freedom from morals as the Neapolitans have.*[75]

While he was at Napoule, Oscar got to know a somewhat neurotic young expatriate Englishman, Harold Mellor (1868–1925), who had inherited a fortune on his father's death five years previously. Mellor had a house at Gland in Switzerland, and invited Oscar to go and stay with him there. Oscar had always been very dismissive of Switzerland, once describing it as *that dreadful place – so vulgar with its big ugly mountains, all black and white like an enormous photograph.* Nonetheless, the offer of free board and lodging was too good to pass up, so he accepted Mellor's invitation. He soon regretted it, as Mellor was a stingy as well as gloomy host, serving indifferent food and even worse wine. While staying in Gland, Oscar received a telegram from Robbie Ross, informing him of his brother Willie's death, at the age of 46. In view of what Oscar called the *wide chasms* that had separated him and Willie for many years, he could not mourn his brother's passing. But it was an unwelcome reminder of his own mortality, adding to the gloom provoked by his current surroundings. As Oscar informed Reggie Turner, *the Swiss are really too ugly . . . life is robbed of its first great element: the people are formless, colourless; one longs for Italy, or England, where beauty walks in the sun.*[76]

England was out of the question, but Oscar did indeed head for Italy when he left Gland at the end of March, unable to bear the place any longer. He tried to extract his rail fare to Genoa from Mellor, but his host refused, so Oscar borrowed it from Mellor's cook instead. At least Italy should be cheap, Oscar informed his publisher Leonard Smithers breezily. *I can live for ten francs a day (boy compris).*[77] At Genoa Oscar visited Constance's grave. Her back condition had steadily worsened, and an operation on her spine was a failure; she had died on 7 April 1898.

Oscar was moved by the sight of the simple cross marking her grave, yet he had to admit that the love he had felt for Constance had died. Despite the heavy cost, not least the loss of his children, he had chosen a different lifestyle, and, as he told several friends, he now believed that a man's love for a male youth could be superior to that of love for a woman. As he was leaving the cemetery, he found a nice new friend with whom to spend the rest of the day.

He nearly always had a good time in Italy, not just because of the easy availability of local youths. There were so many wonderful buildings and so much art to look at. And Oscar was once more flirting with the idea of joining the Catholic Church. It had not escaped his notice that a surprising number of his friends, including Robbie, had converted to Rome. However, Robbie dissuaded him from taking instruction at this time, fearing that Oscar would never be able to take the faith seriously enough for a sustained period. Oscar rather proved his point when he informed Robbie gleefully that he had been kissing a cute young ordinand daily behind the high altar in the Cathedral in Palermo.

A lithograph of Oscar Wilde, posing outside St Peter's in Rome, 1900

Oscar stood in the front rank of pilgrims to Rome during Holy Week in 1900, on a trip paid for by Harold Mellor. He wanted to be sure of getting Pope Leo XIII's blessing, but even the Pontiff was not safe from his mocking humour. Oscar informed Robbie, *I have seen nothing like the extraordinary grace of his gesture, as he rose, from moment to moment, to bless – possibly the pilgrims, but certainly me. {Herbert}*

Tree should see him. It is his only chance. I was deeply impressed, and my walking stick showed signs of budding.[78] Oscar claimed the blessing had helped cure a skin rash he was suffering from, and he went back six times for more. He was also amused one day to see John Gray, now studying at a seminary in Rome, walk past with a group of fellow students; neither of the former lovers said a word.

Most of Oscar's final two years was spent in Paris, however. Having tried various cheap hotels, he found one that suited his needs perfectly: the Hôtel d'Alsace, just down the street from the Hôtel de Nice, where he had started out. The Hôtel d'Alsace (now converted into a very chic and expensive little establishment, called simply l'Hôtel) was not particularly superior in its facilities. But its proprietor, Jean Dupoirier, was an immensely kind man who took it upon himself to try to make Oscar as comfortable as possible, while not worrying too much if he was late in settling his bills. He was not too fussy who Oscar brought back with him, either. M Dupoirier served him a late breakfast in his pair of rooms at the back of the hotel, as well as laying on a regular supply of good but reasonably priced brandy. He would also serve lunch, if required. Usually, however, Oscar would eat out, especially in the evening. When he was able to manage his allowance properly, or a cheque had just arrived, he would often dine at the Café de Paris, only returning in the early hours of the morning. He was not averse sometimes to joining the table of generous foreign visitors, even if this meant that he had to sing for his supper.

Oscar sometimes saw Bosie in Paris, as Lord Alfred spent a good deal of time in France, increasingly at racecourses. The old fire of passion had been damped down, though there was still a mutual recognition of the very special nature of their relationship. When the Marquess of Queensberry died at the end of January 1900, converting to Catholicism on his deathbed, Bosie and his older brother Percy, who inherited the title, came over to Paris together to celebrate. Under the terms of Queensberry's will, the two brothers inherited considerable sums, to do with as they pleased. Queensberry took perverse delight in his conviction that Bosie would squander his share before too long, and he was right – the money went mainly on horses. When Robbie Ross heard that Bosie was, at least temporarily, rich, he urged Oscar to press his case to get a generous settlement from him. Oscar had, after all, spent a small fortune on Bosie in the early 1890s. Bosie's response was characteristic. He informed Oscar that he could not afford to spend anything except on himself, and he told his former benefactor to stop wheedling 'like an old whore'. However, when mutual friends later reprimanded Bosie for not doing enough to help Oscar at the end of his life, he insisted, probably truthfully, that he had, in fact, given him several handouts.

George Alexander, who felt guilty about the fact that he had snubbed Oscar when he first encountered him after his release from prison, made amends by giving Oscar a series of voluntary payments in recognition of the rights he had bought to *Lady Windermere's Fan* and *The Importance of Being Earnest* at the 1895 bankruptcy sale. Moreover, he pledged to bequeath these rights to Cyril and Vyvyan. Even though Oscar was unable to see his sons, he was gratified by the idea that they would benefit in the future from his work, when his plays were once more staged, as they soon were. Robbie Ross had a similar scheme in mind. One of the main motives he had in working to get the bankruptcy discharged on the Wilde estate was that Oscar's sons would benefit, though the debts were not all cleared off until well after Oscar's death.

During 1900, Oscar suffered several prolonged bouts of ill health, which had a serious effect on his good humour. There were periods when he felt reasonably well, and he would enjoy outings to the Paris International Exhibition with sweet Maurice Gilbert. But at other times he just lay in bed feeling wretched. The rashes he had complained about in Rome kept recurring, and their itchiness enraged him. He attributed them to eating bad mussels in the summer of 1899.

More serious were the ongoing problems Oscar was having with his ear. Apart from the fact that he was increasingly deaf, he was often in great pain, and there was an unpleasant discharge. The British Embassy doctor, Maurice a'Court Tucker, who was in frequent attendance at Oscar's bedside from September onwards, recommended an operation, which was carried out by a surgeon in Oscar's bedroom. Worried that his days were numbered, Oscar telegraphed to Robbie in London, asking him to come over, which Robbie faithfully did. Oscar was one of those rather tiresome patients who could seem to be at death's door one moment, then not long afterwards would be chatting merrily away, or even suggesting going out.

Certainly, death was much in Oscar's mind. He had long joked that the British public would never allow him to live into the 20th century, which he considered, correctly, would begin on 1 January 1901. And out of morbid curiosity, he had visited the morgue to see where his body would end up once life had gone. As his condition did genuinely deteriorate from mid-October onwards, he was still capable of gallows humour, declaring famously, while he regarded the rather loud patterns on the walls of his bedroom: *My wallpaper and I are fighting a duel to the death. One or the other of us has to go.* The hotel proprietor used to ease his pain with injections of morphine, but when that ceased to work, the doctor put him on to opium. His last few days were therefore passed in something of a haze, especially when he started drifting in and out of consciousness. Nonetheless, Robbie Ross maintained that towards the very end, Oscar expressed a wish to be received into the Catholic Church at last, though he was unable to speak. He had often said that *Catholicism is the only religion to die in.* An English-speaking priest was summoned, and effectively administered both baptism and the last rites. Early on the morning of 30 November, a death rattle began, but it was not until the early afternoon that the last breath of life escaped. M Dupoirier laid the body out, covered in a white sheet, and Maurice Gilbert took a photograph for posterity. The official cause of death was meningitis.

The monument above Oscar Wilde's grave in Père-Lachaise cemetery in Paris was completed by Jacob Epstein and erected in 1912

Bosie Douglas, summoned by telegram by Robbie, arrived from London two days later, in time to claim his place as chief mourner at the funeral. It was a modest affair, sparsely attended. There was a requiem mass at St-Germain-des-Près, conducted by the priest who had received Oscar into the Church. Only four carriages followed the hearse, the first bearing Bosie, Robbie, Reggie Turner and M Dupoirier. The coffin was cheap and the grave was located in an undistinguished spot of the Bagneux Cemetery. It would be nine years before Robbie was in a position to supervise the transfer of Oscar's remains to the far more suitable Père Lachaise cemetery, where he has a fine tomb, a winged monument designed by Jacob Epstein. Robbie Ross, who also died young, in 1918, arranged that his ashes would be placed in the tomb alongside Oscar.

Bosie Douglas married in 1902 and fathered a son, though the marriage did not last. Bosie became a Roman Catholic, like so many others in Wilde's circle, and renounced his past life. Indeed, for a while he maintained that he had never had homosexual relations with Oscar at all. He became a serial litigant, persecuting Robbie and other 'buggers', before being sent to prison for libelling Winston Churchill. When he died in 1945, he was living with a farming couple in Sussex who had taken pity on his semi-destitute and lonely condition.

Once an outcast because of the way he dared to be true to his nature and defied conventions, Oscar Wilde since his death has become an iconic figure as one of the precursors of the modern age, an individual spirit and a fine craftsman, whose four major plays are still produced around the world, their dialogue just as witty and their social commentary just as sharp as ever.

Notes

Abbreviations used: CLOW: Merlin Holland & Rupert Hart-Davis (eds), *The Complete Letters of Oscar Wilde* (Fourth Estate, London: 2000); OWCH: Karl Beckson, *Oscar Wilde. The Critical Heritage* (Routledge & Kegan Paul, London: 1970); RE: Richard Ellmann, *Oscar Wilde* (Hamish Hamilton, London: 1987);

1   J A Symonds, *Studies of the Greek Poets* (Smith Elder & Co, London: 1873), pp 416–417.
2   Lady Wilde to Rosalie Olivecrona, ?June 1874.
3   Lady Wilde to OW, March 1876.
4   Quoted in OW's 'Mr Pater's Last Volume', *The Speaker*, 12 March 1890.
5   RE, p 45.
6   OW to E F Smyth-Pigott, September 1880, CLOW p 98.
7   W S Gilbert, *Patience* (Chappell & Co, London: 1881).
8   OW to Robert Browning, ? June 1881, CLOW p 111.
9   OW to Oscar Browning, June 1881, CLOW p 111.
10 Henry Newbolt, *My World as in My Time* (Faber & Faber, London: 1932), pp 96–97.
11 OW to the Librarian of the Oxford Union Society, early November 1881, CLOW, p 116.
12 OWCH, p 36.
13 RE, p 138.
14 Letter at the William Andrews Clark Memorial Library, Los Angeles.
15 OW cable, 1 October 1881.
16 *Truth*, 22 December 1881.
17 Like several of OW's most famous quotes, this is impossible to source with certainty.
18 RE, pp 157–158.
19 RE, p 162.
20 *Omaha Weekly Herald*, 24 March 1882.
21 OW to Mrs Bernard Beere, 17 April 1882, CLOW pp 161–162.
22 RE, p 194.
23 JW to OW, 18 September 1882.
24 Robert Sherard, *The Real Oscar Wilde* (T Werner Laurie, London: 1917), p 200.
25 *Punch*, 31 March 1883.
26 Mary Anderson to OW, no date.
27 RE, p223.
28 *New York Times*, 28 August 1883.
29 Constance Lloyd to OW, 11 November 1883.
30 Constance Lloyd to Otho Holland Lloyd, 26 November 1883.

31 OW to Lillie Langtry, ?22 January 1884, CLOW p 224.

32 OW to Harry Marillier, 8 November 1885, CLOW p 267.

33 OW to Harry Marillier, 12 December 1885, CLOW p 272.

34 OW to Robbie Ross, ?18 March 1898, CLOW p 1041.

35 *Pall Mall Gazette*, 16 September 1887.

36 OW to William Ewart Gladstone, ? June 1888, CLOW p 350.

37 Stuart Mason, *Bibliography of Oscar Wilde* (T Werner Laurie, London: 1914), p 334.

38 30 June 1890, 24 June 1890 and 19 July 1890 respectively.

39 George Alexander in the *Evening Standard*, 29 November 1913.

40 OWCH, p 123.

41 OW to Robbie Ross, ?May/June 1892, CLOW p 526.

42 Alfred Douglas to Robbie Ross, 15 July 1896.

43 OW to Alfred Douglas, ?January 1893, CLOW p 544.

44 Max Beerbohm to Reggie Turner, Rupert Hart-Davis (ed), *Letters to Reggie Turner* (Hart-Davis, London: 1964), p 37.

45 RE, p 361.

46 Aubrey Beardsley to Robbie Ross, ?November 1893.

47 RE, p 388.

48 AD to Lady Queensberry, 10 December 1893.

49 RE, p 397.

50 *Pall Mall Gazette*, 1 October 1894.

51 *De Profundis*, CLOW pp 699–700.

52 RE, p 404.

53 OW to Ada Leverson, ?14 January 1895, CLOW p 629.

54 OW to Robbie Ross, ?25 January 1895, CLOW p 629.

55 OWCH, pp 189–190.

56 OW to Alfred Douglas, 17 February 1895, CLOW p 632.

57 OW to Robbie Ross, 28 February 1895, CLOW p 634.

58 OW to Constance Wilde, ?28 February 1895, p 633.

59 Hesketh Pearson, *The Life of Oscar Wilde* (Methuen, London: 1946), p 288.

60 OW to Ada Leverson, 9 April 1895, CLOW p 641.

61 H Montgomery Hyde (ed), *Trials of Oscar Wilde* (William Hodge & Co, London: 1948) p 339.

62 26 May 1895 and RE p 450.

63 *Reynolds's News*, 20 May 1895.

64 Quoted in *De Profundis*.

65 Constance Wilde to Hannah Whithall Smith, 15 October 1895.

66 William Rothenstein, *Men and Memories* 1872–1900 (Faber & Faber, London: 1931), p 311.

67 *New York Times*, 19 May 1897.

68 Ada Leverson, *Letters to the Sphinx* (Duckworth, London: 1930), p 45.

69 OW to the Editor of the *Daily Chronicle*, 27 May 1897.

70 OW to Alfred Douglas, ?31 August 1897, CLOW pp 932–933.

71 OW to Robbie Ross, 21 September 1897, CLOW p 942.

72 Constance Wilde to Arthur Humphreys, 27 February 1898.

73 *Saturday Review*, 12 March 1898.

74 OW to Robbie Ross, 14 May 1900, CLOW p 1187.

75 OW to Robbie Ross, 27 December 1898, CLOW p 1112.

76 OW to Reggie Turner, 20 March 1899, CLOW p 1132.

77 OW to Leonard Smithers, 30 March 1899, CLOW p 1139.

78 OW to Robbie Ross, 16 April 1900, CLOW p 1180.

Chronology

Year	Age	Life
1854		16 October: Birth of Oscar Fingal O'Flahertie Wills Wilde, at 21 Westland Row, Dublin, second son of William and Jane (née Elgee) Wilde.
1855	1	26 April: baptised into the Church of Ireland and christened by his uncle Rev Ralph Wilde, at St Mark's Church, Dublin.
1859	5	Only sister, Isola, born.
1864	10	Sent as a boarder to Portora Royal School, Enniskillen, with his older brother Willie (born 1852).
1866	12	Wins Junior School Prize.

Year	History	Culture
1854	In US, Republican Party founded. Pope Piux X declares the dogma of Immaculate Conception of Blessed Virgin Mary to be an article of faith.	Hector Berlioz, *The Childhood of Christ.*
1855	In Russia, Nicholas I dies; Alexander II becomes tsar (until 1881). In southern Africa, D Livingstone 'discovers' Victoria Falls.	Robert Browning, *Men and Women.* Elizabeth Gaskell, *North and South.* Walt Whitman, *Leaves of Grass.*
1859	Franco-Piedmontese War against Austria. Spanish-Moroccan War (until 1860). Construction of Suez Canal begins (until 1869).	C F Gounod, *Faust.* Wagner, *Tristan und Isolde.* George Eliot, *Adam Bede.* Charles Darwin, *The Origin of Species by Natural Selection.* J S Mill, *On Liberty.* Edouard Manet, *Absinthe Drinker.*
1864	In London, Karl Marx organizes first socialist international. Henri Dunant founds Red Cross. Louis Pasteur invents pasteurisation.	Anton Bruckner, Mass No 1 in D minor. Leo Tolstoy, *War and Peace* (until 1869).
1866	War between Austria and Italy ended by treaty of Vienna. 14th Amendment incorporates Civil Rights Act into US constitution.	Bedřich Smetana, *The Bartered Bride.* Fyodor Dostoevsky, *Crime and Punishment.*

Year	Age	Life
1867	13	Death of his sister Isola.
1870	16	Wins Carpenter Prize for knowledge of the Greek New Testament.
1871	17	Wins scholarship to Trinity College, Dublin, where he studies classics under Rev John Mahaffy.
1873	19	Wins Foundation Scholarship at Trinity College.
1874	20	Wins Berkeley Gold Medal for Greek at Trinity College. June: Passes Oxford entrance examination, winning a Demyship (scholarship) in Classics at Magdalen College. Summer: travels with mother to France and Switzerland. October: begins studies at Magdalen College, Oxford. November: fails Responsions (preliminary exams).
1875	21	23 February: becomes a Freemason, being received into the Apollo Lodge, Oxford. June/July: travels in Italy with Rev Mahaffy. August: Meets first girlfriend, Florence Balcombe.
1876	22	Meets Lillie Langtry for the first time. 19 April: death of Sir William Wilde. June: takes Honour Moderations examination at Oxford (gaining a First). July: returns to Ireland for the summer vacation.

Year	History	Culture
1867	Prussia forms North German Confederation. Austria forms Austro-Hungarian empire. US purchases Alaska from Russia. British North America Act creates Dominion of Canada. Joseph Lister publishes paper on antiseptic surgery.	Giuseppe Verdi, *Don Carlos*. Johann Strauss, *Blue Danube*. Marx, *Das Kapital*. Henrik Ibsen, *Peer Gynt*.
1870	Franco-Prussian War. Papal Rome annexed by Italy. In US, John Rockefeller founds Standard Oil.	Clément Delibes, *Coppélia*. Dostoevsky, *The House of the Dead*.
1871	At Versailles, William I proclaimed German emperor. In Africa, H M Stanley finds D Livingston at Ujiji.	Verdi, *Aïda*. Lewis Carroll, *Through the Looking-Glass*.
1873	In Spain, Amadeo I abdicates; republic proclaimed. In Africa, Ashanti War begins (until 1874). In Asia, Acheh War (until 1903). Great Depression (until 1896).	Arthur Rimbaud, *A Season in Hell*. Walter Pater, *Studies in the History of the Renaissance*. Claude Monet, *Impression: soleil levant*.
1874	In Britain, Benjamin Disraeli becomes prime minister. In Spain, Alfonso XII establishes constitutional monarchy.	Smetana, *My Fatherland*. Richard Strauss, *Die Fledermaus*. In Paris, first Impressionist exhibition.
1875	In China, Kwang-Su becomes emperor (until 1908). Russo-Japanese agreement over Sakhalin and the Kuriles. In Bosnia and Herzegovina, revolts against Turkish rule.	Tchaikovsky, First Piano Concerto in B-flat minor. Georges Bizet, *Carmen*. Mark Twain, *The Adventures of Tom Sawyer* (until 1876). Monet, *Boating at Argenteuil*.
1876	Battle of Little Bighorn; General Custer dies. Alexander Graham Bell patents telephone.	Johannes Brahms, *First Symphony*. Wagner, *Siegfried*. First complete performance of Wagner's *The Ring*.

Year	Age	Life
1877	23	March/ April: travels in Italy and Greece, mainly with Mahaffy. Rusticated by Magdalen College for missing start of term. July: first article published, in the Dublin *University Magazine*. Autumn: *Kottabos*, Trinity College's magazine, prints Oscar's first published sonnet, the gently homoerotic 'A fair slim boy not made for this world's pain'.
1878	24	June: Finals examinations at Oxford. 10 June: learns he has won the Newdigate Prize for his long poem *Ravenna*. July: learns he has been awarded a Double First, but he must return to Oxford for another term to pass compulsory Divinity Examination. November: collects his BA degree.
1879	25	Sharing lodgings in London with Frank Miles, at 13 Salisbury Street, off the Strand. May: mother and brother move from Dublin to London. July: holiday in Belgium.
1880	26	Completes and has privately published his play *Vera*. August: moves with Frank Miles to 1 Tite Street, Chelsea.
1881	27	January: mortgages his inherited hunting lodge at Lough Fee, Ireland. April: Gilbert and Sullivan's *Patience*, satirising aesthetes, including OW, opens in London. June: *Poems* published. July/ August: travels in France. 21 August: Canon Miles decrees that his son Frank and OW must stop living together. 30 September: Richard D'Oyly Carte invites OW to tour America. 3 November: Oxford Union Library returns a presentation copy of *Poems*. 24 December: sails for New York.

Year	History	Culture
1877	Queen Victoria proclaimed Empress of India. Russo-Turkish War. Thomas Edison invents gramophone. In Britain, first Wimbledon tennis tournament.	Emile Zola, *L'Assommoir*.
1878	Congress of Berlin resolves Balkan crisis. Serbia becomes independent. Britain gains Cyprus. Second Anglo-Afghan War (until 1879). In London, electric street lighting.	Tchaikovsky, *Swan Lake*.
1879	Germany and Austria-Hungary form Dual Alliance. In Africa, Zulu War. In south Africa, Boers proclaim Transvaal Republic.	Anton Bruckner, Sixth Symphony. Tchaikovsky, *Eugene Onegin*. Ibsen, *The Doll's House*. August Strindberg, *The Red Room*.
1880	In Britain, William Gladstone becomes prime minister. First Boer War (until 1881). Louis Pasteur discovers streptococcus.	Tchaikovsky, *1812 Overture*. Dostoevsky, *The Brothers Karamazov*.
1881	In Russia, Alexander II assassinated. In Japan, political parties established. Tunisia becomes French protectorate. In Algeria, revolt against the French. In Sudan, Mahdi Holy War (until 1898). In eastern Europe, Jewish pogroms.	Jacques Offenbach, *The Tales of Hoffmann*. Anatole France, *Le Crime de Sylvestre Bonnard*. Henry James, *Portrait of a Lady*. Ibsen, *Ghosts*.

Year	Age	Life
1882	28	2 January: arrives in America at the start of a gruelling lecture tour that takes him all over the United States and Canada. 18 January: visits Walt Whitman. 21 January: meets Henry James, who finds OW 'repulsive and fatuous'. 28 January: meets Henry Wadsworth Longfellow. 8 September: meeting with the actress Mary Anderson, to discuss a new play he has in mind, *The Duchess of Padua*. 23 October: greets Lillie Langtry off her ship in New York. 27 December: sails for London.
1883	29	February to May: based in Paris, working on the *Duchess of Padua*. Meets Victor Hugo, Paul Verlaine, Stéphane Mallarmé and Emile Zola, among others. Mid-May: returns to London, where he starts to court Constance Lloyd. August: in New York for the unsuccessful premiere of *Vera*. September: begins British lecture tour. 25 November: Becomes engaged to Constance Lloyd.
1884	30	29 May: wedding of OW and Constance, followed by a month's honeymoon in Paris and Dieppe. August: stands in for his brother Willie as drama critic for *Vanity Fair*. December: the 'House Beautiful' at 16 Tite Street takes shape.
1885	31	January to March: another lecture tour, including over 20 engagements in Ireland. 20 February: James McNeill Whistler attacks OW in a public art lecture. 5 June: birth of the Wildes' first son Cyril. 27 November: visit to Cambridge, to see young admirer Harry Marillier.
1886	32	Some time during the year, OW is seduced by the 17-year-old Robbie Ross. ?5 November: birth of Wildes' second son, Vyvyan.
1887	33	11 May: 'Lord Arthur Savile's Crime' begins serialisation in the *Court and Society Review*. 17 July: OW elected a Fellow of the Society of Authors. November: assumes editorship of *Woman's World* (formerly *Lady's World*).

Year	History	Culture
1882	Fenians murder new Irish chief secretary, Lord Frederick Cavendish, and T H Burke, Irish under-secretary, in Phoenix Park, Dublin.	Manet, *Le Bar aux Folies-Bergère*. Wagner, *Parsifal*.
1883	Jewish immigration to Palestine (Rothschild Colonies). Germany acquires southwest Africa. In Chicago, world's first skyscraper built.	Antonín Dvořák, *Stabat Mater*. Robert Louis Stevenson, *Treasure Island*.
1884	Sino-French War (until 1885). Berlin Conference to mediate European claims in Africa (until 1885).	Jules Massenet, *Manon*. Mark Twain, *Huckleberry Finn*. Georges Seurat, *Une Baignade, Asnières*.
1885	Belgium's King Leopold II establishes Independent Congo State. In Transvaal, gold discovered. Gottlieb Daimler invents prototype of motorcycle.	Zola, *Germinal*. Guy de Maupassant, *Bel Ami*.
1886	In Cuba, slavery abolished. In India, first meeting of National Congress. In Canada, Canadian Pacific Railway completed.	H Rider Haggard, *King Solomon's Mines*. Stevenson, *Dr Jekyll and Mr Hyde*. Rimbaud, *Les Illuminations*. Leo Tolstoy, *The Death of Ivan Ilich*.
1887	In Britain, Queen Victoria celebrates Golden Jubilee. Heinrich Hertz produces radio waves.	Verdi, *Otello*.

Year	Age	Life
1888	34	May: publication of *The Happy Prince and Other Tales* to favourable reviews. 31 August: OW's brother Willie declared bankrupt.
1889	35	Affair with John Gray begins. July: 'The Portrait of Mr W H' appears in *Blackwood's Magazine*, outraging some critics.
1890	36	June: *The Picture of Dorian Gray* appears in *Lippincott's Magazine* (July issue), to even greater opprobrium. August/September: holiday in Scotland.
1891	37	26 January: *Guido Ferranti* (the retitled *Duchess of Padua*) opens for a short run in New York. February: *The Fortnightly Review* publishes *The Soul of Man under Socialism*. Early March: visit to Paris. April: revised book version of *The Picture of Dorian Gray* published. June: Lord Alfred Douglas taken by Lionel Johnson to meet OW. 12 July: meets Aubrey Beardsley for the first time. 4 October: Willie Wilde marries a rich American widow, Mrs Frank Leslie. November: *A House of Pomegranates* appears to good reviews. November/ December: back in Paris, meets André Gide, Marcel Proust and others.
1892	38	20 February: *Lady Windermere's Fan* opens at the St James's Theatre, the first of his four successful social comedies. ?April: Lord Alfred Douglas seeks OW's help in dealing with a blackmailer. June: rehearsals of *Salomé* (with Sarah Bernhardt in the lead role) begin at the Palace Theatre in London, but the production is cancelled when it is banned by the Lord Chamberlain. July: in Bad Homburg, Germany, on a health cure. August/September: in Cromer, Norfolk, working on *A Woman of No Importance*.

Year	History	Culture
1888	In Germany, William II becomes emperor (until 1918). In Asia, French Indo-China established. In Brazil, slavery abolished.	N Rimsky-Korsakov, *Scheherezade*. Rudyard Kipling, *Plain Tales from the Hills*. Strindberg, *Miss Julie*. George Eastman invents the first commercial roll-film camera: the 'Kodak' box.
1889	Second socialist international. Italy invades Somalia and Ethiopia. In Paris, Eiffel Tower completed.	Richard Strauss, *Don Juan*. Verdi, *Falstaff*. George Bernard Shaw, *Fabian Essays*.
1890	In Germany, Otto von Bismarck dismissed. In Spain, universal suffrage.	Tchaikovsky, *The Queen of Spades*. Paul Cézanne, *The Cardplayers*. Ibsen, *Hedda Gabler*.
1891	Building of Trans-Siberian railway begins. Shearers' strike in Australia.	Tchaikovsky, *The Nutcracker*. Henri Toulouse-Lautrec, *Le bal du Moulin-Rouge*. Paul Gaugin goes to Tahiti.
1892	In the UK, W E Gladstone becomes prime minister. The Panama scandal breaks in France and Ferdinand de Lesseps is committed for trial for corruption and mismanagement.	Monet begins picture series of Rouen Cathedral. R Leoncavallo, *I Pagliacci*. M Maeterlinck, *Pelléas et Mélisande* with C Debussy's music.

Year	Age	Life
1893	39	February: in Torquay with Alfred Douglas and his tutor. 22 February: French text of *Salomé* published in London and Paris. OW in Paris for launch. March: staying at the Savoy Hotel in London. Rent boy Alfred Wood tries to blackmail him. 19 April: *A Woman of No Importance* opens at the Haymarket Theatre. Early May: visits Alfred Douglas in Oxford. Late May: in Paris, Pierre Louÿs breaks off friendship with OW over his treatment of Constance. June/September: most of the summer spent writing at The Cottage at Goring-on-Thames. 11 December: *A Woman of No Importance* opens in New York.
1894	40	January: Willie Wilde, divorced and back from the United States, marries Lily Lees, at a ceremony boycotted by OW. 9 February: English translation of *Salomé* appears, with illustrations by Aubrey Beardsley. March: goes to Paris to join Alfred Douglas, who has spent the winter in Egypt. May: OW and Alfred Douglas run into André Gide in Florence. 11 June: limited edition of *The Sphinx* published. 30 June: back in London, OW receives an unexpected call from the Marquess of Queensberry. August/September: based at a rented house in Worthing, writing *The Importance of Being Earnest*. Early October: staying in Brighton with Bosie, who becomes ill, as then does OW. 16 October: OW's 40th birthday, marked by a poisonous letter from Bosie.

Year	History	Culture
1893	Franco-Russian alliance signed. South Africa Company launches Matabele War. France annexes Laos.	Dvořák, *From the New World*. Tchaikovsky, *Pathétique*.
1894	In France, President Carnot assassinated. Uganda becomes British protectorate. In France, Alfred Dreyfus convicted of treason. In Russia, Nicholas II becomes tsar (until 1917).	Claude Debussy, *L'Après-midi d'un Faune*. Gabriele d'Annunzio, *Il trionfo della morte*. Kipling, *The Jungle Book*. G B Shaw, *Arms and the Man*.

Year	Age	Life
1895	41	3 January: *An Ideal Husband* opens at the Haymarket Theatre. Late January early February: in Algeria with Bosie. 14 February: *The Importance of Being Earnest* opens at the St James's Theatre. 18 February: Queensberry leaves a libellous message at Oscar's club; he only picks it up 10 days later. 1 March: warrant for Queensberry's arrest issued. 3–5 April: Queensberry's libel trial. 5 April: warrant for OW's arrest issued and executed, with the prisoner being taken to Holloway. 24 April: Queensberry forces a bankruptcy sale of the contents of the Wildes' house. 26 April–1 May: first trial of OW and Alfred Taylor, ending with the jury failing to reach a verdict. OW released on bail. 20–25 May: second Wilde trial, ending in a guilty verdict. Early June: moved to Pentonville Prison. 4 July: transferred again, to Wandsworth Prison. 21 September: Constance, now living abroad, visits OW in prison. 12 November: appearance before bankruptcy court. 21 November: while being transferred to Reading Gaol, is humiliated at Clapham Junction station.
1896	42	3 February: death of Lady Wilde. 11 February: *Salomé* opens in Paris. July: Major James Nelson becomes the new Governor of Reading Gaol. 7 July: Charles Wooldridge hanged in Reading Gaol for the murder of his wife.
1897	43	January-March: composes the long letter to Bosie that will become *De Profundis*. 1 April: appoints Robbie Ross to be his literary executor. 18 May: final transfer, back to Pentonville. 19 May: released from jail and travels to France. 26 May: settles in Berneval, near Dieppe, writing *The Ballad of Reading Gaol*. 28 August: OW and Bosie reunited, at Rouen. Late September: rents a villa in Posillipo, near Naples, with Bosie.
1898	44	January: lingers in Naples, though Bosie and he have split up. February: *The Ballad of Reading Gaol* is published and sells well. Oscar has meanwhile moved to Paris. 7 April: Constance dies in Genoa, after a spinal operation. December: OW goes to the south of France, where he remains for three months, partly at Frank Harris's expense.

Year	History	Culture
1895	Japan conquers Taiwan (Formosa). Lumière brothers invent the cinematograph. Guglielmo Marconi invents wireless telegraphy. Wilhelm Röntgen invents X-rays.	H G Wells, *The Time Machine.* W B Yeats, *Poems.*
1896	Theodore Herzl founds Zionism. First olympic games of the modern era held in Athens. Antoine (Henri) Becquerel discovers radioactivity of uranium.	Giacomo Puccini, *La Bohème.* Thomas Hardy, *Jude the Obscure.*
1897	In Britain, Queen Victoria celebrates Diamond Jubilee. Britain destroys Benin City. Klondike gold rush (until 1899). J J Thomson discovers electron.	Joseph Conrad, *The Nigger of the Narcissus.* Stefan George, *Das Jahr der Seele.* Strindberg, *Inferno.* Edmond Rostand, *Cyrano de Bergerac.*
1898	Spanish-American War: Spain loses Cuba, Puerto Rico and the Philippines. Britain conquers Sudan.	Henry James, *The Turn of the Screw.* H G Wells, *The War of the Worlds.* Zola, *J'Accuse.* Auguste Rodin, *The Kiss.*

Year	Age	Life
1899	45	March: in Gland, Switzerland, as a house-guest of Harold Mellor. 13 March: death of Willie Wilde. April: in Italy. May: returns to France. August: installed in the Hôtel d'Alsace, Paris, his final home.
1900	46	31 January: death of the Marquess of Queensberry. March: ill with food poisoning. April: visits Italy with Harold Mellor. 10 October: has an ear operation in his hotel room. 30 November: dies in the presence of Robbie Ross and Reggie Turner.

Year	History	Culture
1899	Second Boer War (until 1902). Aspirin introduced.	Hector Berlioz, *The Taking of Troy*. Edward Elgar, *Enigma Variations*. George, *Der Teppich des Lebens*.
1900	First Pan-African Conference. In France, Dreyfus pardoned. Relief of Mafeking. In China, Boxer Rebellion (until 1901). First Zeppelin flight.	Puccini, *Tosca*. Conrad, *Lord Jim*. Sigmund Freud, *The Interpretation of Dreams*.

Further Reading

A sure route to bankruptcy is to try to acquire every book about Oscar Wilde and his circle. Most are out of print and some are expensive collectors' items, but there are a number of what one might consider core works.

The most substantial biography, in every sense of the word, is Richard Ellmann's *Oscar Wilde* (Hamish Hamilton, London: 1987, but frequently reprinted). This book was a true labour of love, but Ellmann's deteriorating health during the latter stages of the project undoubtedly led to the fact that he gave scant coverage to Oscar's final years, after his release from prison. There are also quite a number of errors, including a rather startling caption to a photograph of the Hungarian opera singer Alice Guszalewicz playing Salome, which claims that this is Oscar in drag. Many of the errors have been identified and written about, with Teutonic thoroughness, by the German scholar Horst Schroeder.

Ellmann is refreshingly candid about Wilde's sexuality, in comparison with some earlier and slighter lives, but there is a whole host of more recent books that pursue this aspect of the subject with vigour and, sometimes, imagination. Neil McKenna's *The Secret Life of Oscar Wilde* (Century, London: 2003) is the most provocative, presenting some fascinating evidence of Wilde's erotic escapades, as well as a considerable amount of speculation. On a more academic level, Alan Sinfield's *The Wilde Century: Effeminacy, Oscar Wilde and the Queer Movement* (Cassell, London: 1994) offers some valuable insights from a modern 'queer studies' standpoint.

Several of Oscar's friends wrote memoirs of him, not least Frank Harris, whose *Oscar Wilde* (Bretano's, New York: 1916; Robinson, London: 1997) is at times scurrilous and inventive, but nonetheless more revealing and accurate than has sometimes been acknowledged. André Gide's slim volume *Oscar Wilde* (William Kimber, London: 1951, translated by Dorothy Bussy and Justin O'Brien) is particularly evocative, though it was roundly condemned by Lord Alfred Douglas as fanciful. Douglas's own writings on Wilde – notably *Oscar Wilde and Myself* (John Long, London: 1914) – are a morbidly fascinating exercise in self-justification, laced with vitriol.

Oscar was more fortunate with his descendants. Though frustratingly devoid of dates and index, Vyvyan Holland's *Son of Oscar Wilde* (Rupert Hart-Davis, London: 1954) is an often moving account of the Wilde legacy. Vyvyan Holland also published a pictorial biography of his father, *Oscar Wilde* (Thames and Hudson, London: 1960), which was later mirrored by an attractive volume by his own son, Merlin Holland: *The Wilde Album* (Fourth Estate, London: 1997). Building on earlier work by Rupert Hart-Davis, Merlin Holland also edited an updated version of Wilde's correspondence, *The Complete Letters of Oscar Wilde* (Fourth Estate, London: 2000), which provides perhaps the best exposition of the subject's character of any single volume, though it is a weighty proposition at over 1,200 pages.

Oscar's family have themselves been the subjects of several books, including Terence de Vere White's *The Parents of Oscar Wilde* (Hodder and Stoughton, London: 1967), Joy Melville's *Mother of Oscar* (John Murray, London: 1994) and Ann Clark Amor's *Mrs Oscar Wilde: a woman of some importance* (Sidgwick and Jackson, London: 1983). Oscar's niece, Dolly, was portrayed in somewhat idiosyncratic fashion in Joan Schenkar's *Truly Wilde: the unsettling story of Dolly Wilde, Oscar's unusual niece* (Virago, London: 2000). Oscar's principal male lovers have similarly been placed under close scrutiny. Lord Alfred Douglas's most recent full-length portrait was Douglas Murray's *Bosie* (Hodder and Stoughton, London: 2000). Robert Ross's latest outing was my own *Robbie Ross* (Constable, London: 2000).

Countless editions of Wilde's plays and prose writings are readily available, as well as selections of his much loved 'wit and wisdom'. The Oxford University Press is bringing out, at a sedate pace, the complete Wilde oeuvre in academically useful but costly volumes; John Sloan's *Oscar Wilde* (Oxford University Press: 2003), in the cheaper Authors in Context series, is recommended. Cambridge University Press produced a valuable collection of academic essays, edited by Peter Raby, *The Cambridge Companion to Oscar Wilde* (1997). Anne Varty's *A Preface to Oscar Wilde* (Longman, London: 1998) admirably fulfils her publisher's claim to provide a scholarly and critical study 'intended for those needing modern and authoritative guidance through the characteristic difficulties of [the author's] work to reach an intelligent understanding and enjoyment of it.'

Understanding and enjoyment, in equal proportion, are also at the heart of the publications and activities of the Oscar Wilde Society, whose journal, *The Wildean*, superbly edited for many years by Don Mead, provides both stimulation to Wilde scholars and enlightenment to Oscar enthusiasts. Enquiries to the Oscar Wilde Society, 100 Peacock Street, Gravesend, Kent DA12 1EQ.

List of Works

Acknowledgements

Extracts from *The Complete Letters of Oscar Wilde*, edited by Merlin Holland and Rupert Hart-Davis, Fourth Estate, London, 2000, are reprinted by permission of HarperCollins Publishers Ltd.

Picture Sources

The author and publishers wish to express their thanks to the following sources of illustrative material and/or permission to reproduce it. They will make proper acknowledgements in future editions in the event that any omissions have occurred.

Akg-Images: pp. 39, 87, 89, 124, 129; Getty Images: p. 51; Mary Evans Picture Library: pp. 14, 36, 46; National Library of Ireland: pp. 6, 7, 10; Rue des Archives/Lebrecht Picture Library:pp. i, ii, 19; Topham Picturepoint: pp. 21, 22, 26, 35, 42, 50, 54, 65, 85, 96, 99, 103, 107, 128.

Index